T0059392

Voudon Gnosticism

"With chapters on Leghba, the Lord of Sexual Magic, the Voudonist Kabbalah, the Work of OTOA and LCN, and working with Les Vudu, the author presents a comprehensive introduction to practices within the tradition. He appreciates the central dictum that the magician is an artist and should continually explore their own inner kingdoms, led by what they find there. Many who enter this tradition, even those without professed artistic ability, suddenly find themselves driven to produce works. In this way, the Hoodoo manifests in current time and space, drawing sustenance from these objects as if they were offerings. Frater Vameri has made an offering of his own, one that others may take a piece of and, nurturing it, find their own journey into the realm of Voudon Gnosticism. It will help them gain a clearer understanding of Michael Bertiaux's work and perhaps reveal their own secret identity as a lucky Hoodoo."

SEAN WOODWARD, GRAND MASTER OF
ORDO TEMPLI ORIENTIS ANTIQUA AND
AUTHOR OF *KEYS TO THE VOUDON KINGDOM*

"Finally, we have a book that explains the framework of Bertiaux's magical world with clarity and simplicity, providing invaluable context and meaning to his magical world."

KATY DE MATTOS FRISVOLD, COAUTHOR OF
THE CANTICLES OF LILITH

VOUDON GNOSTICISM

An Introduction to the Rites and Practices

FRATER VAMERI

Destiny Books
Rochester, Vermont

Destiny Books
One Park Street
Rochester, Vermont 05767
www.DestinyBooks.com

Destiny Books is a division of Inner Traditions International

Cataloging-in-Publication Data for this title is available from the Library of Congress

ISBN 978-1-64411-927-3 (print)
ISBN 978-1-64411-928-0 (ebook)

Printed and bound in the United States by Lake Book Manufacturing, LLC
The text stock is SFI certified. The Sustainable Forestry Initiative® program promotes sustainable forest management.

10 9 8 7 6 5 4 3 2 1

Text design by Virginia Bowman and layout by Kenleigh Manseau
This book was typeset in Garamond Premier Pro with Spirits Soft used as a display font

To send correspondence to the author of this book, mail a first-class letter to the author c/o Inner Traditions • Bear & Company, One Park Street, Rochester, VT 05767, and we will forward the communication, or contact the author directly at **www.eduardoregis.com**.

I dedicate this book to Les Vudu,
who typed all these words with me.
I also dedicate it to my initiator Frater Selwanga
and to the great explorer of universes
known by the earthly name of Michael Bertiaux.

Contents

Gnostic Vûdû: An Introduction

Nicholaj de Mattos Frisvold

On the evening of July 6 in 1974, a most interesting conjunction took shape: the sun, Saturn, and Mercury all lined up in the sign of Cancer together with Vulcanus and Sol Niger, an intense conjunction known as the Gate of Man. This astrological moment occurs when the solstice moon opens the watery veil of summer between the worlds so humans can traverse into the realms of hidden mysteries with greater ease, a perfect moment for spirit contact made possible. That night, Michael Bertiaux and Lucien François Jean-Maine gathered in the home of Marc Lully along with four other people to conduct a séance. This was one of many séances these seven people of the inner circle of mysteries had conducted, but the spirit teacher who communicated in this séance emphasized two elements of great importance for Gnostic Voudon. First, how the Voudon Gnostic priesthood was a mystical type of priesthood, a priesthood that would continue the work of Jules Doinel, who founded the Église Gnostique in 1890. But Doinel's work was judged merely to be an awakening. The mystical priesthood gathered at the table in Lully's apartment were called to work with not only the aeon or Christo-Logos of Doinel but also with the daemon. This would take the form of a "new image of the Afro-Atlantean religion and its philosophy, the new order of the Vûdû faith-experience, and the new gnosis of reborn oracles."[1] This new form of Vûdû saw Legba as the aeon propagated by Doinel, hence Legba-Christ was established as the aeon that would complement the Ghuedhe family of *lwas* or spirits as the daemon in this syzygy under the banner of esoteric Voudon, or Gnostic Vûdû. Here we find a perfect balance between the two luminaries of heaven, the sun and the moon, through the family of Legba and the family of Ghuedhe.

This mystical priesthood was represented by artist-magicians, semi-otic shamans, and occult researchers, or as Bertiaux writes in his *Voudon Gnostic Workbook*: "The gnostic artist is a magician when he allows the divine energy of creative and cosmic illumination to enter into his multidimensional consciousness and thus awaken the angels of their inspiration."[2] In order to assist in this work, the Gnostic artist has as his road map—or if a culinary metaphor is welcome, his cookbook—Michael Bertiaux's 1988 publication *The Voudon Gnostic Workbook*.

This work was completely different from anything preceding it, and I recall the day when I got my copy of this doorstop of a book, which I had found hidden away on a shelf filled with scarfs and crystals in a store in Oslo selling clothes, incense, and imported Asian products. The bookseller had hidden the book because of the terrible word *Voudon* in the title, which, the cashier told me, everyone knew was associated with evil. If only he had bothered to open the book and read the contents he would have found chapter 9, which states that the purpose of the magician is "to hold back the powers of evil." Anyway, I am digressing. This was in 1992, and in search of a guide that would help me understand *The Voudon Gnostic Workbook*, I discovered the works of Kenneth Grant, in particular Grant's *Cults of the Shadow* (1975), a profound piece of writing, which was a most welcome read.

Like Bertiaux, Grant can be difficult to access as he is also working within the realm of Gnostic artistry, not the least his own esoteric logomachy of the Kabbalah. The pursuit of understanding Bertiaux's magical system is bound to bring on frustration and confusion as *The Voudon Gnostic Workbook* is not an orderly system of rules and instructions but is designed for the Gnostic explorer, the Hoodoo man to discover his or her own system or, more precisely, magical ontology. Readers who are in search of a logical and orderly system—not the esoteric logic that Bertiaux uses to compose and manifest these lessons and teachings—discard this masterpiece. It is also important to keep in mind that Bertiaux's work, his teaching organ, the Monastery of the Seven Rays, and his orders, Ordo Templi Orientis Antiqua (OTOA) and La Couleuvre Noire (LCN), or the Black Snake Cult, are at root spiritualist and hence teachings given from other intelligences are pivotal. This is evident in how so many lessons in *The Voudon Gnostic Workbook* are attributed to the spirit teacher giving the teachings and lessons.

Another element of importance is philosophy. Bertiaux is presenting a magical ontology through the lenses of Heidegger, Bergson, and Husserl, which means that he is inviting us to explore an almost infinite number of states of being in order to find resonance and reference. His workbook is written to assist in these efforts. Hence his writings involve the explorations of strange landscapes, whether they be the City of Fa, Meon or B-Universe, or the Zothyrian Empire, which will ultimately unlock potential or wisdom in the ontological sphere of the Gnostic artist.

The exploration of multiple universes finds its occult physics in the tantric doctrines discussing *chakra* and *loka*. Chakras are, as we know, power centers in the human body that when activated will trigger access to a given loka, or world. The findings of the saddhus and tantric sages, like Gorakhnath, concerning the existence of many worlds and even worlds within worlds that stretch across time and space, are similar to the discoveries of Niels Bohr and Werner Heisenberg in the 1920s, what we today know as quantum mechanics.

The Voudon Gnostic Workbook is divided into four parts. The first part deals with Voudoo energies, the second with Gnostic energies, the third with elemental sorcery, and the last with elemental theogony. The latter part is concerned with the elements necessary for the construction of the "mystical and gnostic being."

This being said, *The Voudon Gnostic Workbook* is not a readily accessible work. So far, the books *Keys to the Hoodoo Kingdom* by Sean Woodward (2017), *Syzygy: Reflections on the Monastery of the Seven Rays* by Tau Palamas (2013), and *Hoodoo Pilot* by Kyle Fite (2020) have been great works to consult in getting a clearer understanding of Bertiaux's universe. Frater Vameri's book joins these other works in contributing to a greater understanding of Bertiaux.

Vameri, also known as Eduardo Regis, starts from the Franco-Haitian roots of OTOA and LCN, namely in the work and person of Martinez de Pasqually (1727–1774) and the influence of his Ordre des Chevaliers Maçons Élus Coëns de l'Univers on Bertiaux. From here the Franco-Haitian connection is explored through Papus and Lucien François Jean-Maine, leading to the early fusion of Voudon with several of the mystical and theurgic streams found within the larger French Gnostic tradition. With this as a backdrop, Regis discusses central themes in *The Voudon Gnostic Workbook*, giving special attention to the essential and important first lessons in the first part of the workbook, which are known as lucky Hoodoo. That along with ample discussions on the Zothyrian mysteries and the Ghuedhe mysteries becomes the backbone of this book. In this way, Regis connects the Gnostic and Vodouist elements into a passionate and clear presentation of Voudon Gnosticism, which adds in a great way to the slowly growing library of books expounding upon this complex and beautiful new vision of the Vûdû faith.

Nicholaj de Mattos Frisvold is a psychologist, anthropologist, and writer who has conducted extensive studies in African and Afro-derived religions and sorcerous cults. He has published several works on these topics and has had personal involvement with several of these faiths, notably Ifá, where he is a member of the prestigious council of elders, the Ogboni Society. He is a Grand Master of O.T.O.A., a Baille-Ge/Hierophant of L.C.N., and the Abbot of The Monastery of St. Uriel the Archangel, located in Brazil. His published works include *Palo Mayombe* (2010), *Pomba Gira* (2011), *Exu* (2012), *Ifa: A Forest of Mystery* (2016), *Trollrún* (2021), and *Seven Crossroads of Night: Quimbanda in Theory and Practice* (2023).

Preface

In this book I talk about magic, spiders, spirits, strange boxes, H. P. Lovecraft, and much more. What do all of these have in common? Me, of course. Confused? It will all become clear pretty soon. First, let me tell you all about who I am, how this book came to be, and why I think you should read it.

The work you now have in your hands is the result of a selfish effort. Almost everything I have written in these pages I wrote to either organize my ideas or communicate with Frater Selwanga, the person who initated me into these practices. Once I realized what I had written, I changed some passages to include a broader audience and continued to write with those readers in mind.

You might be wondering who I am and why you should make the effort to read this book. After all, why should you pay attention to any of my words? I will let you be the judge of whether you should continue reading or put this book down. I can, however, provide some information that might help you make your decision.

I have been dabbling in the occult and spirituality for quite some time now. You might or might not have stumbled upon some of my previous work (signed as Eduardo Regis, my birth name) published in some anthologies and books, some in English, some in Portuguese, about magic and Afro-American religions. In my home country of Brazil I have been working within the Golden Dawn system for a while and also in other traditions, such as Martinism, Haitian Vodou, Umbanda, and Quimbanda. I have also been involved with the Voudon Gnostic tradition by means of the Ordo Templi Orientis Antiqua (OTOA).

It is within the scope of the OTOA and of Voudon Gnosticism that this work falls. It is no accident that I have dedicated an entire book to this tradition: I consider it to be important and transformative. I started my work on the Voudon Gnostic system and the OTOA with Frater Selwanga some years ago, and pretty soon it became evident that I was about to face a challenge. What OTOA and Frater Selwanga asked of me was to find my own magical universe within, to organize it, and to discover and tangle with its own powers and abilities. Easy? By no means. But imagine, with me, the rewards of these efforts. Imagine the discoveries, insights, and marvels that lie ahead for those who set themselves this task. It is a truly alchemical and magical journey.

For example, it was by means of the work in the Voudon Gnostic system that I have uncovered a very old link of mine with spiders—and should you decide to keep on reading this book you will learn a little bit about that part of my work. Also, my exploration of my very own magical veins and bones has revealed to me some great insights about how magic works and especially how magic works specifically for me. Given that we are all very different persons and beings, why should magic work the same for all of us? It makes sense that it should work a little differently for me than for you, right? It makes sense that some magical symbols, triggers, and rituals should be more appealing to me than to another magical practitioner. Of course, we have known that for a while now, hence the many magical traditions that have evolved. But even within the same tradition there should be enough space for variations.

The Gnostic system I write about here is plastic: it can accommodate a variety of individuals and coherently unite many different ideas and currents. On the other hand, it has a very solid structure and logic behind it. Through the reasoning and all the mechanisms of this system one can unfold many new magical powers and really go deep within discoveries and achievements. It is indeed a system for people who want to dive into this ocean of magical possibilities.

This book is a compilation of the magical work I have done for the last few years and an example of what I have achieved through Voudon Gnosticism. It is meant to be an introduction, a guiding hand. But it is also a product of my own magic. No one else could have written this book. Not because it is perfect or superior to others, but because it is a reflection of who I am—and the mirror I have used to achieve what I present here to you in the pages of this book. That is why I decided to sign the book as Frater Vameri—my magical motto at OTOA—to show that this book is the result of a work made possible because of the instructions and support I found in the Voudon Gnostic system.

This book was not planned: it just happened. While I was writing it I realized I could share what I had understood so far and so pave a way for those seekers who do not know Voudon Gnosticism that well or for those who have tried to get to know the system but felt intimidated by the complexity of its seminal works, such as *The Voudon Gnostic Workbook* by Michael Bertiaux.

There are few books about Voudon Gnosticism, and the majority of them were not written with the beginner in mind. It was my plan to turn this book into a portal to Voudon Gnosticism that readers could pass through and come out the other side knowing a bit more about Voudon Gnosticism and the OTOA.

Maybe you have just opened this book in a bookstore or are reading a preview on a website and have no idea about what Voudon Gnosticism is or who Michael Bertiaux is and what he has to do with this magical system. I present a detailed discussion about the history of OTOA and talk a great deal about Bertiaux in this book, but let me just summarize: Bertiaux traveled to Haiti where he was initiated in OTOA. He returned to the United States and began to teach the order's magical system, which ultimately came to be known as the Voudon Gnostic system. In its roots, OTOA is a blend of different magical and mystical currents with a good dose of Haitian Vodou and Gnosticism, hence the name Voudon Gnosticism. It is imperative to understand, though, that Voudon Gnosticism is not equal to Haitian Vodou and never claimed to be one and the same with that beautiful religion.

I have just stated that the Voudon Gnostic system is not a religion, and that has become a great source of confusion for some. Because of the word *Voudon*, many are ready to assume that this system is some kind of *corruption* of Vodou, but this is a wrong assumption. Voudon Gnosticism was born from Haitian Vodou, as a kind of esoteric tradition practiced by some Haitian mystics and sages, but it is definitely not that religion or any religion. In short, this is not a book about any kind of religion. In its essence, this is a book about magic. Magic and religion are sometimes hard to separate, but here we have a case where this difference is more pronounced.

I have written this book assuming that the reader is familiar with some of the more common magical ideas, notions, and content. This is a book for magicians: all of them. If you are interested in the occult and have never heard of this system, I really think you will like what this book can show you. If you are one of those who has heard about OTOA and Voudon Gnosticism and thought it was all nonsense, well, I also invite you to read this book. Maybe you keep your opinion (who knows?), but at least you will be more knowledgeable about the system.

I think it is pretty clear by now that though this work started out as a selfish act it soon evolved into a gift from me to readers. I do not intend to say that I am enlightened or a great master. I am neither. I am just a guy who studied and did some pretty interesting experimentations and thought about sharing his point of view with others. I believe we would have a healthier and more vibrant occult community if people started to share what they have experienced and what they know.

I present here a set of texts that, in addition to talking a lot about me, hopefully also talks about the Voudon Gnostic system in a clear manner. May those interested in this system find my words and may they help them.

Finally, I wish to leave you with this invocation that I suggest you read right now, before you go any further:

As I stand before this portal, I ask Les Vudu to shine their light.
There is no darkness that I cannot penetrate.
The path is now clear ahead, stones, sticks, vipers, and bones all set.
There is no poison or fear that can turn me away.
I am the alchemist.
I am the mage.
I am the Hoodoo man (woman).
I am the Voudon man (woman).
As Legbah-Moses by the power of Damballah opened the sea,
I now activate all the heat and thunder inside me.
As it is my right I claim as mine the eye of Odin.
I am one with Les Vudu and I feel their magic within!

Happy reading and happy travels.

FRATER VAMERI

1
The Foundation: History and Myth

Many myths are origin stories. They provide structure for a society. It is important that we keep this in mind as we go through this chapter dealing with the foundational myth of the Voudon Gnostic system. Even before discussing what Voudon Gnosticism itself is, we must go into an archaeomythical excavation to discover its fundamental pillars, so that when it comes time to define this system we can do so successfully. This approach may seem a bit misleading but trust me: it is just what we need now so that we can clearly understand the chapters that follow.

Maya Deren has written that myths constitute "twilight speech." Honestly, this is one of the best definitions ever coined. A myth is, in fact, a story of passage from one state to another, from the earlier to the later, and as such, it is always caught in an in-between state. What could that mean? Now, by being in an environment that is always liminal, a myth is ambiguous: it embodies truths but the events described may never have occurred; it is reality but also fiction. However, this does not mean that a myth does not have certain characteristics that are set in stone. Yes, myths have them, and the main characteristic, I would say, is this: myths are always true!

Confusing? Not so much. It does not matter where exactly in the myth fictional or factual elements enter. Determining what is fact and what isn't will, in most cases, be a useless and even deleterious exercise, unless done for scientific purposes, of course. When something enters the mythical category, it takes on legitimacy and, therefore, becomes a structuring truth.

This does not mean that we should suspend our criticism or start believing in anything in our daily lives. The message here is slightly different—to understand and experience whatever the myth structures we will need to understand it as true, without reservation. That is what we must do from now on, because the myth that I will present over the following pages is, like all myths, full of mysterious characters and events whose unique accounts are those passed on from mouth to ear. It's a rich and interesting myth that travels the world and brings together an unlikely group of people and cultural elements, and we need to follow these connections carefully to achieve the ultimate goal of this book.

This myth is a story, of course. It is a story that will culminate in the Voudon Gnostic system as we know it today. If we were to really look for its beginning, we would get lost in the murky waters of a very distant past. Therefore, I chose to start it from a definite point well known to those interested in the Western esoteric tradition. Come along with me.

Our story begins with one of the most enigmatic figures in the Western esoteric tradition, a man who played a very important role, especially in the French occult scene. His name was Jacques de Livron Joachim de la Tour de la Casa Martinez de Pasqually, born probably in 1727 and almost certainly dead in 1774. Some say he was Portuguese, others say he was Spanish, and there is no shortage of other theories about his nationality. Some even claim that he was Jewish, but opponents of this theory are full of arguments against it. Truth be told: where he was born and his ethnicity are of very little interest to us. Martinez de Pasqually,* as he became better known, appears continuously and

---

*Different spellings can occur, for example, Martines de Pasqually.

Image 1.1. Martinez de Pasqually, Reproduction of a portrait found in *Le diable au XIXe siècle ou, Les mystères du spiritisme* (1893) by Léo Taxil. Public domain.

prominently in the history of esotericism and of French Freemasonry. His most celebrated contribution, without a doubt, is the founding of the L'Ordre de Chevaliers Maçons Élus Coëns de l'Univers (Order of Knights Masons Elected Priests of the Universe) in 1761. The teachings and philosophies of Élus Coëns have strongly influenced Martinism, and the order remains active to this day, revived by Robert Amberlain in the mid-twentieth century.

Pasqually's great work is undoubtedly *The Treatise on the Reintegration of Beings*, a challenging book that presents a complex discourse about the Creation and Fall of man. Although it is beyond the scope of this book to discuss the entire philosophy of his treatise,* we can say that it deals with how to reverse the Fall, thus promoting the reintegration of humanity to its original state and status, which to us may even seem divine.

---

*For that I do recommend Ivan Côrrea's excellent book *Teodicéia Psíquica* (2020), which has a chapter that summarizes Pasqually's philosophy. Unfortunately, this book is still only available in Portuguese.

Pasqually never completely finished outlining his ideas because of his untimely death in 1774. Pasqually's death is also surrounded by mysteries, mainly because of his departure from France a few years earlier. It so happens that in 1772, Pasqually traveled to the colony of Saint-Domingue, which would become Haiti in the early nineteenth century, under the pretext of claiming an inheritance.* Precise details here are as scarce as they are in most of Pasqually's history, but we do know that he founded Élus Coëns temples in Saint-Domingue.

We will return to Saint-Domingue and to Haiti later, but now, the boat we are steering in this story must do what Pasqually never did: return to France.

We need to speak now of an extremely popular and far less mysterious figure than Pasqually: Louis Claude de Saint-Martin (1743–1803), also known as the Unknown Philosopher. He was born in Amboise, France, and was raised in an environment dominated by the Catholic creed. His father sent him to study law, a course that he completed, but the profession of lawyer did not appeal to him and he had no interest in practicing it. Because of his family connections, he ended up joining the army. However, evidence suggests that he was quite unfit for the service. The story goes that his health was always fragile, something that would certainly not match the military life. Either way, Saint-Martin eventually studied the humanities and went on to become a full-fledged philosopher. It was in 1767 that the paths of Saint-Martin and Pasqually crossed, precisely because Saint-Martin's military regiment was stationed in Bordeaux, where Pasqually had also settled that year.

---

*I have heard an oral report that Pasqually went to Saint-Domingue to learn the mysteries of the Vodou religion and that the entire inheritance story is a lie. According to my informant, Pasqually was very interested in the magical technology of Vodou, which allowed practitioners to enter in direct contact with the spirits. Also, this informant told me that Pasqually died because of the result of some dangerous magical operations.

Image 1.2. Louis Claude de Saint-Martin, 1801.
Portrait by Jean-Baptiste Fouquet and Gilles-Louis Chrétien.

Saint-Martin joined the Élus Coëns between August and October 1768, and we know that Pasqually's philosophy and wisdom vigorously influenced him. In fact, he worked as Pasqually's secretary until 1771, the year in which he left the army and began to dedicate himself only to his spiritual and mystic affairs. The period of close contact between Pasqually and Saint-Martin suggests that the former strongly shaped the latter's ideas. However, when Pasqually left France in 1772, Élus Coëns suffered a shock: after the abrupt loss of its director, the organization entered a state of confusion. This must have been essential for inducing Saint-Martin, a gifted and dedicated mystic, to begin to walk his own path.

In the year of Pasqually's death, Saint-Martin was already firmly on his own trail and was writing his book, *Of Errors and Truth*, in Lyon. In addition to Pasqually, Saint-Martin was later deeply impressed with and influenced by the works of Emanuel Swedenborg and Jakob Böhme, and he used a lot of the ideas of these authors to establish his own original thoughts. In fact, we know that it was only in 1788 that

Saint-Martin came to know the works of Böhme, who became perhaps the most important figure in Saint-Martin's initiatic life, as stated by Saint-Martin himself.*

In 1798, the Spanish Inquisition condemned *Of Errors and Truth*. We need to remember that Saint-Martin was brought up under strong Catholic influence. Furthermore, he never strayed from the church during his lifetime. Saint-Martin most likely had great affection for the institution and for the doctrine of Catholicism. For this reason, Arthur Edward Waite states in his biography of Saint-Martin that he believes that this conviction was a severe blow and that it may have contributed to the decline in his health, which culminated in his death in 1803.

Saint-Martin left other written works and influenced a number of important figures in esotericism. Our next character is one of those people touched by Saint-Martin, and we need to talk about this great occultist, since his participation in our myth is central.

It was in Spain, more precisely on July 13, 1865, that our next character was born, the son of a Spanish mother and a French father. We're talking about Gérard Encausse (1865–1916), better known as Papus. In his youth, Encausse showed great interest in the occult, reading and studying the books he found in libraries, including the works of Éliphas Lévi. He was also a member of the Theosophical Society, the Hermetic Brotherhood of Light, and the Hermetic Order of the Golden Dawn in Paris.

In 1880, Henri Delaage, one of Saint-Martin's disciples, initiated Papus into his master's teachings. In 1884, Papus met Augustin Chaboseau (1868–1946), and the two realized that they both had initiations from the Saint-Martin lineage and decided to form the Martinist Order, based on the latter's philosophy. In 1888, together with Chaboseau and Stanislas de Guaita† (1861–1897), Papus

---

*I do not discuss Swedenborg and Böhme in more detail, but I do recommend their works.
†Another author whose works are recommended. De Guaita wrote a treatise about diabolism and especially condemned the practices of Eugène Vintras (1807–1875) and Joseph-Antoine Boullan (1824–1893). Curiously, those two figures influenced the Voudon Gnostic current, in particular Boullan, who is considered one of its masters.

founded another order: the Cabalistic Order of the Rosy-Cross.

Encausse also attended medical school, graduating in 1894, and had a very successful career as a physician. In addition to his regular visits to patients, he edited a homeopathy magazine and worked as a homeopath for Russian Tsar Nicholas II and his wife, the Empress Alexandra. Encausse also wrote several treatises on medicine, although these are certainly not as famous as his esoteric books.

M. le Dʳ ENCAUSSE (Papus)
Médecin de l'Hôpital Saint-Jacques.

Image 1.3. Gérard Encausse, Papus. Portrait by unknown artist, date unknown. Courtesy of *Bibliothèque interuniversitaire de santé* via Wikimedia France, June 23, 2017.

Even while really busy with his medical practice, it seems that Encausse, or rather Papus, kept occultism as his main occupation, given his long initiatory curriculum and his vast production of tomes in the area. It was in 1908, during the International Masonic Conference, that Papus met Theodor Reuss (1855–1923), although Papus himself was never a regular Freemason. Reuss was the leader of the Ordo Templi Orientis (OTO) before it was taken over by Aleister Crowley (1875–1947) and subjected to the law of Thelema, the esoteric and occult spiritual philosophy founded by Crowley. The story goes that, following this meeting, Papus was recognized as a X° (tenth degree) initiate of the OTO.

Regarding the OTO, it is interesting to point out that it is famous for its initiatory degrees dedicated to sexual magic. In fact, we know that Theodor Reuss widely propagated the notion that members of the order were the keepers of the secrets of this type of magic. However, what is less well known is that these secrets very likely find their foundation in the teachings of Paschal Beverly Randolph and in the instructions codified in the Hermetic Brotherhood of Luxor and in the Hermetic Brotherhood of Light.

In 1916, while Papus was serving as a doctor in the First World War, he became infected with tuberculosis in a field hospital. Papus could not resist the disease and died on October 25 of the same year.

These three figures we've discussed in brief will blend together impressively in the story of another haunting personality, a man named Lucien François Jean-Maine (1869–1960). Not as well known as the men discussed so far, Jean-Maine is, however, also the root of a very interesting initiatic lineage. To understand this figure better, we need to go back in time and take a look again at Pasqually's journey to the colony of Saint-Domingue.

Saint-Domingue was a French colony, and when Pasqually arrived there in 1772, the place was a huge enterprise. Sugar and coffee plantations exported their products all over the world, enriching the French settlers while the enslaved Africans who provided all the labor were treated as a disposable part of the colonial machinery.

Despite being oppressed, these enslaved Africans resisted as best they could, either with revolts or by creating surprising cultural traditions. Coming from the most diverse places in Africa, but with special emphasis on the Kingdom of Congo, the Yoruba nations, and the speakers of Gbe, these men and women were forming their own and very interesting spirituality on the island, which would come to be known as Haitian Vodou.

One of the great centers of Saint-Domingue was Leógâne, in the south of the colony. There, Martinez de Pasqually had founded one or more temples of Élus Coëns. Although we don't know exactly how, Lucien François Jean-Maine's family members were initiated into these temples. Here, the suspicion about how this initiation would have occurred is justified by the fact that blacks, even freedmen, did not usually find it easy to be accepted in Masonic lodges, which leads us to think that it would also not be simple to obtain initiations into other orders as well. Either way, Jean-Maine's family members manage to be initiated, and after Pasqually's death, they and others founded an order known as Les Templiers Noirs.

As soon as Martinism began in France, it spread to Haiti (Saint-Domingue became the independent Haiti in 1804). Thus, Jean-Maine grew up under the influence of the teachings of Pasqually and Haitian Vodou and later became acquainted with Martinist philosophy. Jean-Maine was made *houngan*, or priest, of Vodou by his own father. In addition, he studied Haitian Masonic rites, including a rite that would have been propagated by the revolutionary Toussaint L'Ouverture (1743–1803), with influences from Kabbalah and African cosmogonies. Jean-Maine also studied Paschal Beverly Randolph's esoteric currents and his sex magic techniques and was consecrated a Gnostic bishop.

In 1910, Jean-Maine traveled to Paris and met Papus. The latter raised him to the X° (tenth degree) of the OTO. Papus, in turn, received from Jean-Maine other initiations and exchanged lineages with him. Some say Jean-Maine made Papus a houngan of Haitian Vodou. I know that this last piece of information may surprise many, especially those who know Papus only through the Martinist bias. However, it is imperative to remember that Papus was quite eclectic, as is Martinist doctrine itself.* In addition, he was also most likely involved with Roma magic from his mother's family.

After that, Jean-Maine was stranded in Europe because of the First World War and other problems. He ended up spending time in Spain and finally returned to Haiti in 1921, where he soon got married. In the same year he founded the Ordo Templi Orientis Antiqua (OTOA), which combined teachings from the OTO of Reuss, Vodou, and other esoteric currents. In 1922, Jean-Maine created another order, La Couleuvre Noire (LCN), an internal order, but sister to the OTOA and more focused on deeper mysteries of the Voudon Gnostic system. His son Hector was born in 1924, and after Jean-Maine's death in 1960, Hector was consecrated Gnostic bishop and became grand master of the OTOA in 1962.

Our founding myth now invites another important character and perhaps the one that will be discussed the most from now on. Michael Paul Bertiaux was born in 1935 in Seattle, Washington. It is worth noting that his mother was a prominent theosophist in the local community and that his father was involved with Buddhism. In other words, he grew up in a home with diverse spiritual influences. Also, it is important to note that his mother, Bernice, was an artist and that she awakened in Bertiaux his talent for painting, which would be so important in his occult work and comprehension in the future.† In 1963,†† Bertiaux traveled to Haiti as an Episcopal pastor to teach philosophy, but history took him in other directions. In fact, Bertiaux met Hector Jean-Maine††† and was initiated by him that very same year into the OTOA, LCN, and other mysteries. More than just initiating Bertiaux, Jean-Maine showed him the work of Haitian artists who produced art inspired by their contact with spirits, and this made a deep impression on Bertiaux.

---

*Martinists reading this should remember the teachings of the initiate grade.
†As Ariock Van de Voorde reveals in his interview with Bertiaux at the Fulgur website.
††Some sources state that this all happened in 1964. But according to Bertiaux's reports in his book *Vûdû Cartography*, it seems more likely to have happened in 1963.
†††Some report that there was also a second initiator called Carlos Adhémar.

Image 1.4. Michael Bertiaux and Hector Jean-Maine. Portrait by Diógenes Costa.

When he returned to the United States after his trip to Haiti, Bertiaux severed ties with the Anglican Church, moved, and devoted himself to the Theosophical Society. Afterward, Bertiaux ended up diving deeper into the initiations passed by Jean-Maine when the latter was forced to reside in the United States because of the dictatorial regime in Haiti. When Jean-Maine arrived in the United States, he contacted Bertiaux and invited him to paint some spiritual entities, and so Bertiaux started to develop his own very unique way to make contact with the invisible world.

It was through Bertiaux that the magical system that began with Lucien François Jean-Maine gained ground all over the world. The first relevant publication in this regard was *Lucky Hoodoo*, a short course in voudoo power secrets, in 1977. Bertiaux signed this publication with the pseudonym Docteur Bacalou Baca.*

---

*Bacalou Baca (Bakalou Baka) is a very aggressive spirit of Vodou. It is usually advised that people keep their distance from him because of his ferocity.

However, it was really through the publication in 1988 of *The Voudon Gnostic Workbook* that both Bertiaux and the Voudon Gnostic system won the world. As soon as it was released, *The Voudon Gnostic Workbook*—a huge collection of lessons about the philosophy and system—caused all sorts of reactions. The fact is that, to this day, no one who reads it stays indifferent to it.

Bertiaux is the central figure in several orders, Gnostic churches, and schools of occultism. Bertiaux astonished the great Kenneth Grant (1924–2011) with his original and challenging thoughts and concepts. However, Bertiaux's influence was not restricted to occult circles and reached even pop culture, as can be seen in Grant Morrison's comic book series *The Invisibles*, which deals, among other things, with magic and presents several concepts typical of Bertiaux's work.

At the time of writing this book, Bertiaux is active—writing, painting, and promoting movie nights where the occult meaning of the picture is discussed. One of Bertiaux's most curious methods of work, heavily documented in books such as *Vûdû Cartography* and *Ontological Graffiti*, is a kind of spiritist session held with entities where he and others conduct interviews and gain inspiration from the spirits. These contacts inspired Bertiaux to paint thought-provoking pictures of these entities. Photos and videos of his apartment reveal walls and hallways filled with these magical, hypnotic canvases. According to Bertiaux himself, his paintings and those of others are a legacy of Haitian occultism itself, in which he and his cohorts express the complex and abstract ideas of their experiences through art.[1]

Now that we have an overview of the myth and understand where Voudon Gnosticism came from, we can move on to answering the question of what, in fact, this system is.

2

What Is the
Voudon Gnostic System?

It is possible that the vast majority of people who come across Bertiaux's *Voudon Gnostic Workbook* (VGW) wonder what it is all about. Truth be told, the aforementioned book is a gem, but it is not very welcoming to beginners or to those who are not familiar with all the premises and influences of both Bertiaux and Jean-Maine. Questions about this work can start with the title itself: What is, after all, a Voudon Gnostic? What is Voudon Gnosticism?

Especially for those who do not read English, but even for those who do, finding solid and clear information about the Voudon Gnostic system is a difficult task. To be fair, books have been published about the subject, but some have been out of print for some time, in addition to propagating a very particular view of Bertiaux. Others are focused on some specific aspects of the system and do not present a greater overview. Thus, a more introductory explanation about the Voudon Gnostic system is opportune and necessary and, hopefully, will attract new people to it and encourage those who have strayed from the VGW, because they couldn't understand some of its concepts, to return to it.

I would like to offer, then, an initial explanation about the Voudon Gnostic system, needed as a basis for our work in this chapter. In a nutshell: Voudon Gnosticism is a magical system built from different influences and based on the construction of a unique magical reality. It is important to make it clear at the outset that Voudon Gnosticism is not synonymous with Haitian Vodou. It is evident that this understandable confusion exists. The Voudon Gnostic system has its roots in Haitian Vodou, but it is built on top of these foundations and is not to be confused with this religion or spirituality. So, let it be noted: we are not discussing Haitian Vodou here, and Voudon Gnosticism should not be confused with it.

Within the Voudon Gnostic system, practitioners work with the *lwas*, the central spirits of Haitian Vodou. However, these spirits are approached from another perspective and under other premises. The magical work within the Voudon Gnostic system with a certain lwa is not the same as working with said lwa within Haitian Vodou. Having experience in the Voudon Gnostic system does not make anyone a Haitian Vodou priest! This must be repeated: initiations in the Voudon Gnostic system or even success in magical operations within this system do not make anyone a *serviteur* (servant) of the lwas or a priest of Haitian Vodou. It is necessary that we keep these two practices separate. For color versions of the images below, see color plate 1.

Image 2.1. A Vodou ceremony in Port au Prince, Haiti. Although the Voudon Gnostic system presents similar themes, these typical manifestations of Haiti are not part of this system.
Photos by Fritz Rudolf Loewa.

Image 2.2. A Vodou ceremony in Jacmel, Haiti.
Photo by Doron. See also color plate 2.

In fact, when we start to distill the other influences of the Voudon Gnostic system, as they present themselves in the VGW, we see that we are dealing with something unique. The influence of the Hermetic Order of the Golden Dawn, Thelema, Shintoism, and Nordic spiritualities, to name a few elements, on Voudon Gnosticism is notorious. Thus, we are faced with an effervescent cauldron of many ingredients that may seem a big mess at first glance but which later reveals itself to have great cohesion. As the saying goes: "Whoever has eyes to see, let him see."

Perhaps the most important element in understanding the cohesiveness of the system is its plasticity. This is precisely why it is difficult to see how much Voudon Gnosticism has coherent connections. Plasticity gives the system in question the eclectic and syncretic flavor that, for many, is just an uncompromising mixture of preferences and experimentation. However, if we change this perspective and start to see plasticity as an aggregator of layers, meanings, and connections that are built by the individual within his subjective universe, we realize that it is the spirit of Bertiaux himself that is being mirrored in the system outlined in the VGW. With that in mind we realize that, therefore, we can also face our own reflection in this same mirror.

In other words, whoever enters this system and hopes to fully understand and use it needs to become the architect of his own subjective universe without any fear of getting his hands dirty in the process. However, I feel that maybe we are getting a little ahead of the discussion and maybe it would be more prudent to return to what Bertiaux presents, always taking the VGW as a reference.

It is no exaggeration to say that the system presented in the VGW is complete and that it, in itself, is a source of endless experiments and experiences.* Vodou and its lwas are only part of this set, but we can understand that the name Voudon was not chosen (or, at least, did not end up being popular) by chance and that, more broadly, it represents several characteristics of the system in question, such as the mixture, the meeting of apparently disparate elements that talk to one another under a special perspective, and the fact that the interaction with spirits is one of the pillars of the practices suggested in the VGW.

The first part and perhaps most famous section of the VGW deals with the lucky Hoodoo grimoire and, right away, suggests that the practitioner make a pact with the spirits of Hoo and Doo, setting a certain tone for the book and the system. Here, we are faced with an important choice: the use of the term *Hoodoo*. The aforementioned term is very often confused with the term *Voodoo*—an English spelling for Voudou, which is being substituted for the more appropriate spelling Vodou.** The term *Vodou*, sometimes spelled *Voudon*, derives from *Vodun*, which originated with the Gbe speakers of Africa. However, Hoodoo is a magical system created by enslaved African Americans in the southern United States and was also built on the strong influence of African

---

*The totality of the system is, however, distributed among the Monastery of the Seven Rays and other documents.

**For a good overview about the differences among Vodou, Voodoo, and Hoodoo, I recommend the book *Vodou, Voodoo, and Hoodoo: Explore the Evolution of Caribbean Magic* by Sébastien de la Croix and Diamantino Fernandez Trindade (2024).

spiritualties, cosmogonies, and philosophies, as well as Christianity and Christian esotericism.

Thus, Hoodoo is like a brother to the Voudon Gnostic current, and so it is not surprising that the two are intimately linked in the system Bertiaux revealed to the world. We will talk about the *lucky Hoodoo*, the Hoodoo encarnation that figures in the VGW, in more detail in chapter 5, as it is the gateway to the system in general. I hope the reader is noting how we are slowly building a better idea of what the Voudon Gnostic system is through this exercise of associations and expansion of concepts, but let's continue. We are not yet finished with the task.

Throughout the VGW, Bertiaux takes you through different concepts, locations, and mythologies. We depart from Atlantis, go to the dark corners of H. P. Lovecraft and his myth of Cthulhu, and even find ourselves facing other planets and empires that dominate alternate universes, such as the Zothyrian Empire. This almost sci-fi flavor is further proof of the plasticity and complex subtlety of the Voudon Gnostic system. If we interpret everything that is put in the VGW literally and objectively, we will certainly be getting lost in a labyrinth—the key is to aim at the subjective and let the processes that are beyond rationality act in all their richness.

This variety of subjects and concepts presented in the VGW, as we have already seen, can seem chaotic. In fact, everything there is sewn together and is part of a great universe built by Bertiaux. We could argue that his work deserved a more careful literary edition, but what we cannot say is that everything that is there is not part of a common root. We could also argue that the name Voudon Gnostic is not the most appropriate for such a diverse myriad of elements. Well, names don't go away that easily, and this one, like it or not, is already well established. We'd better stick with it for now. Later on, I hope to be able to convince you that this terminology is, in fact, perfect.

We are already stretching for a few pages to answer a simple question. This reveals that the question is not that elementary and that the answer is somewhat elusive. However, as we walk through this discussion, we are being introduced to notions that will accompany us throughout this work.

Note that a key term has appeared more than once so far. I'm referring to *subjective*. More specifically, we have already spoken twice about the *subjective universe*. What this means is that Voudon Gnosticism is not a system that feeds on different random influences but on different influences that make part of the imaginative and abstract constitution of the operator, the magician, the Voudon Gnostic. So the metaphor I presented earlier of the mirror reflection is appropriate. Bertiaux looks at Voudon Gnosticism and sees in it a system that reflects himself. If we do the same exercise, we will have a distinct image, one that reflects ourselves—if we know just how to see it!

Perhaps we are ready, after all, to formulate a more complete conceptualization of the Voudon Gnostic system. It is a magical and subjectively constructed system that allows the operator to edify, reveal, and control universal forces through contact and knowledge of spirits and intermediaries. It is a Gnostic system, as it is concerned with knowledge of the invisible through living experience. It is Voudon, as it's an organic, dynamic blend that has its roots also in African American philosophies and an emphasis on spirits, remembering that Vodun in its original sense means something similar to spirit.

Now, we have a more powerful conceptualization, but one that is perhaps still a little abstract for those who do not know the system from the inside—that is, for those who have no experience with it. Well, nothing replaces practical experience and living the system, but we can try to paint a more complete picture in the next chapter as we discuss exactly what is done within the Voudon Gnostic system. After all, often the definition of something encompasses pretty much the activity promoted by that thing or carried out by the professional in that area. We will see if this approach can help us.

3
Becoming a Voudon Gnostic

What do Voudon Gnostics do anyway? Or even, what makes someone a Voudon Gnostic? Answers vary, of course. Allow me, however, to offer my perspective. You may agree or disagree with my point of view, but I consider it highly unlikely that the suggestions I will make here will not be of use somehow to those interested in the system in question.

The most obvious would be to state now that the Voudon Gnostic is the one who works within the Voudon Gnostic system. Simple and straightforward as that. However, what exactly does that mean? Such a direct approach only brings us back to the original trouble spot, so we need to be more specific. Let's go deeper.

To become a Voudon Gnostic, you must dive in search of the Atlantean ruins and open portals to Zothyria while talking to the lwas and summoning the icy wind from Odin's chariot. It is necessary to be a tree that bears different fruits without losing its identity, and it is necessary to have very strong roots for this to be possible. For instance, a Yggdrasil who is also a Gran Bwa (Great Wood in a direct translation, but we must also keep in mind that Bwa can mean penis), is a Haitian lwa associated with wild trees and plants. The Voudon Gnostic is a challenger and a skillful builder who must tear the veil of illusion and see behind it, see the mechanisms, spirits, and angels engaged in their routine and structuring work. He must recognize that there is a part of divinity in himself and claim this power and make it his very own.

It is not easy to be successful in the office of the Voudon Gnostic, but the reward is abundance and enrichment. Just as Rome was not built in a day, no one can become familiar with and fit into the Voudon Gnostic system in a short time. Therefore, here are some suggestions that may help those who wish to take on this challenge.

Learn a little bit about Haitian Vodou through proper sources. Well, I have already strongly insisted here that Voudon Gnostic is not Haitian Vodou. At the same time, I hope it has become crystal clear that the second influences the first. Thus, it is important and will help tremendously to know a little about Haitian Voudou, its rites, lwas, and customs. It is important, however, to realize that it will not make sense and will not be desirable to try to emulate Haitian Voudou while working with the Voudon Gnostic system. Without any reservations, I can say that Voudon Gnosticism is built upon Haitian Vodou but not to identify with it. It is not a copy.

Finally, to familiarize yourself with Haitian Vodou, I suggest my book *Vodou Haitiano: Serviço aos Lwas* (2022) and also *Vodou, Voodoo, and Hoodoo: Explore the Evolution of Caribbean Magic* by Diamantino Fernandes Trindade and Sébastien de la Croix (2023), the first of which is only in Portuguese for now. Also, I recommend the book *Serving the Spirits* by Mambo Vye Zo Komande LaMenfo (2011) and *Haitian Vodou* by Mambo Chita Tann (2012).

Studying the different religious manifestations of the world without reservation is also an important exercise. Knowing, at least superficially, Eastern and Western religions will help you to understand some nuances of Bertiaux's writings and of the system. I know this suggestion seems abstract—at least, it's broad—but we're talking about something that must be built over a lifetime and without any rush.

Devour all reliable material about religious movements, especially those that influenced Gnosticism (like the Manichaeans), which will be discussed briefly in chapter 8. There is no way to put a list of suggested readings here or it would take up endless pages, but always look for books by university professors, recognized intellectuals, or religious leaders. Avoid falling into the trap of reading books that are propagandist or full of misinformation. Don't forget to study African and Afro-American religions in addition to Haitian Vodou.

I recommend reading the following books by Nicholaj de Mattos Frisvold: *Exu and the Quimbanda of Night and Fire* (2016), *Palo Mayombe: The Garden of Blood and Bones* (2016), and *Pomba Gira and the Quimbanda of Mbumba Nzila* (2011). I also recommend *The Formation of Candomblé: Vodun History and Ritual in Brazil* by Luis Nicolau Parés (2013), *The Invention of God* by Thomas Römer (2015), *Traditional Brazilian Black Magic* by Diego de Oxóssi (2021), anything written by Mircea Eliade, the Bhagavad Gita, the Dhammapada, and any papers on Manichaeism.

Since we touched on the subject, let's talk about studying and getting to know the Gnostic movements properly. Some may not realize the importance of Gnosticism within the Voudon Gnostic system, but it is really important to know the different Gnostic movements. Again, this is a task that will require long hours and years, but we cannot be in a hurry. The history and philosophy of the Gnostics are diverse and complex. Contrary to what many imagine, there is no single and homogeneous Gnosticism. In fact, *Gnosticism* is a term used to encompass a variety of spiritual practices and philosophies typical of early Christianity. These different practices or cults were so diverse that some researchers even wonder if the term is adequate or if it causes more confusion than clarity.

Familiarity with these early Christian systems can only be achieved through reading several books about them. Again, don't be in haste. Study calmly and move on. I recommend starting with *Forbidden Faith: The Secret History of Gnosticism* by Richard Smoley (2007), and his selected bibliography will guide you to other books to study. Also, don't forget to check *Gnosticism: New Light on the Ancient Tradition of Inner Knowing* by Stephan A. Hoeller (2002).

It is necessary to have a solid and wide base of esotericism and occultism if we want to go deep into Voudon Gnosticism. Knowing even a little about theosophy, French esotericism (Martinism, mesmerism, and Éliphas Lévi), the English school (Hermetic Order of the Golden Dawn and Thelema), and also the works of Paschal Beverly Randolph and mystical Kabbalah will be of great value.

I am not proposing that one become an expert in all these currents: that would be absurd. However, it is not possible to overlook the fact that the knowledge based on these movements will be extremely valuable. To that end, I recommend reading the books by Lévi, Louis Claude de Saint-Martin, Papus, H. P. Blavatsky, Charles Webster Leadbeater, Israel Regardie, Chic and Tabatha Cicero, Aleister Crowley, P. B. Randolph, Dion Fortune, and Lon Milo Duquette. In summary, I strongly recommend that you read everything you can from these authors and from other great names in esotericism that were left out here for the simple fact that it is impossible to formulate an exhaustive list.

Study the different movements and thinkers of Western philosophy. Bertiaux is an author extremely versed in the different philosophical movements, and he often adopts certain concepts derived from those when expressing himself, and he does not warn us about this, as he assumes that the student of Voudon Gnosticism is already familiar with such conceptualizations. So it will be extremely rewarding to get to to know some of the philosophers. Dive into Platonism, Neoplatonism, and all the more modern philosophers like Nietzsche, Heidegger, and others. Also don't shy away from studying psychology and the works of Freud and Jung, just to name the most famous ones.

Of course, some of these texts can be extremely complicated and indigestible for those who do not have training in the humanities. There are, therefore, several introductory books written by professors and researchers that aim precisely to present the philosophy of these thinkers to the general public. There is no shame in using this resource. In fact, most serious students of philosophy also needed help at the beginning. So there is no reason for us to be different. Remember that the key idea here is to understand the principal concepts formulated by those thinkers and not to master their ideas and writings. Books that offer an overview of the most significant philosophers should be more than enough for a jump-start.

Finally, it is necessary to study diligently everything that can be found that was written by Bertiaux. Recently, some years of studies of the Monastery of the Seven Rays, which is the body of teachings of the OTOA, was published and made available to the general public. This complete course is divided into four years and contains several fundamental elements for an accurate understanding of the Voudon Gnostic system. However, the complete materials will probably be only available to OTOA members. As not everyone will want to join OTOA and it is not necessary to do so in order to work with VGW, although it helps a lot, I recommend reading *Monastery of the Seven Rays: First Year Course* (2019) and the subsequent years available. In addition, other books, such as the aforementioned *Vûdû Cartography* and *Ontological Graffiti* and others by Bertiaux are recommended. Together, they will make up a more seamless scenario. Be on the lookout for new material by Bertiaux, as he continues to write and recently published a three-volume series entitled *Cagliostro: The Secret Lives* (2021–2022).

Of course, this list of suggested topics for reading and studying is neither exhaustive nor a mandatory prerequisite. Many will immediately begin working with the Voudon Gnostic system while still studying these myriad subjects. The practical part should never be put in the background because it will, in fact, promote the most complete understanding of the system.

This discussion about practice, by the way, deserves a little more attention. Over the years I've noticed that many interested in the occult are dedicated to collecting books and more books. However, only a small portion of these persons take the trouble to study these volumes. Of this small group, an even smaller number engage in something of a practical nature.

It is evident that there is no issue or problem with being a book collector or a dedicated student of the occult as a theoretical science. In fact, scholars are invaluable when they set out to produce material to share with the world, as they offer their unique and strongly informed perspectives. However, the Voudon Gnostic cannot be merely a scholar or a secondhand book dealer. If he does so, he will be already failing to be a de facto Voudon Gnostic.

The message here is straightforward: you have to get your hands dirty and "burn your fingers."

Practice is the only way a mage does magic. Everything else is something else.* The magic proposed by the Voudon Gnostic system is personal and its purpose is to access spirits, realms, and dimensions that are very specific to the operator or practitioner. When talking about something so intimate, it is necessary to note that experience is fundamental and irreplaceable. Experience has the power to shape the paths we follow and to reveal to us the recesses of our individuality and subjectivity. Through living, experiencing, feeling, and being impressed and moved, we trigger processes that will enable us to slowly understand and put our magical universe in place.

By writing this, I do not intend to diminish the importance of reasoning, intellectual investigation, or intellectual unveiling; on the contrary, they are important tools. But if the student only engages in intellectual activity, he will deprive himself of necessary experiential learning. He will not become aware of the worlds and entities that surround him and will not get on his own path to becoming a Voudon Gnostic.

I commented at the beginning of this section that the Voudon Gnostic launches himself on the Atlantean continent, and as I have already highlighted, it is necessary to understand this subjectively. I

---

*I recall the excellent book *Jonathan Strange & Mr Norrel* by Susanna Clarke, which makes a satire on this issue—although I don't know if she had actual magicians in mind when she wrote it. In the book there is a society of magicians who do not do magic. They only study it because, after all, it would be absurd to do magic.

would like to take this idea as an example. Imagine that you read everything possible about Atlantis. Certainly, you will build a relatively well-defined idea about what this mythical place would have been like. This construction is in a purely intellectual or rational dimension, but it can be expanded or further worked on or rediscovered through practical experience.

In the case at hand, following our example, let us now imagine that you feel willing to actually get to know Atlantis and, as Athanasius Kircher did in his exploration of Mount Vesuvius, decide to actually go there. According to the magical processes and operations that we know, this is not only entirely possible but it's not as complicated as it sounds. Then, after a magical ritual, you set out on a journey through the astral realms and arrive at the lost continent. Through the use of creative imagination or visualization, powerful weapons of the Voudon Gnostic, you will be able to see and feel, touch and interact with the continent. Now, wouldn't this be a very rich experience and completely different from a mere intellectual construction?

The beauty of these magical experiences is that, in addition to providing these fantastic adventures, they reveal doors, characters, and paths never imagined by us. Who knows, for example, who you will meet on your journey to Atlantis? And what will these explorations reveal about you?

Well, if Atlantis doesn't suit you, don't worry—there are infinite locations and realms in the multiple dimensions of reality. The Voudon Gnostic will have access to all of them. That's right—all of them.

Now, surely some readers will be wondering if all a Voudon Gnostic does is travel and explore realities of being. The answer is no. In fact, nothing that is possible through magic (i.e., everything) is beyond the reach of this mage.

The Voudon Gnostic learns to speak with spirits and obtain important revelations, information, and teachings from them. Not only that, he also learns to awaken truly world-altering powers. We will see in the next chapter some of the things that are taught in the VGW, but we can say here that the Voudon Gnostic system allows, for example, for attracting luck and influencing events and people. Exactly what the operator will do with these capabilities is up to the individual.

In accessing other universes, such as the B-Universe or Meon, the great ineffable and unimaginable nothing, the Voudon Gnostic can have indescribable and never-before-imagined experiences. He goes, literally, beyond the Mauve Zone to the trans-Yuggothian recesses and from there extracts power and knowledge. Under the auspices of Baron Lundi or even the arachnid lwas, he can make infinite journeys and transforms himself into an astral spider that will wander through the threads of existence.

So what does a Voudon Gnostic do? He seeks gnosis, pulsating knowledge. He drinks from the fountain of living water that gushes out of the cosmic Yggdrasil and that fills the sea into which Damballah-Odin plunges on his shamanic journey. He launches UFOs and *ojas* into the air and other types of Voodoo radioactivity while program-

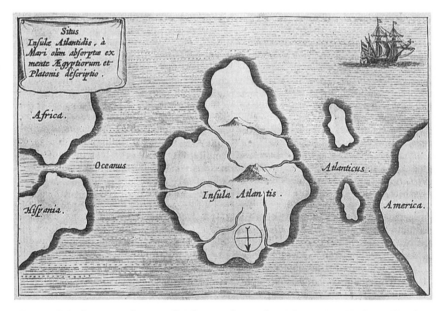

Image 3.1. Suggested map of Atlantis, drawn by Athanasius Kircher after he ventured into the crater of Mount Vesuvius.
Source: Athanasius Kircher, *Mundus Subterraneus* (1678).

ming Voodoo computers in stellar temporal stations, in twisted nebulae inhabited by Afro-Atlantean mysteries.

He sits in his temple, a powerful esoteric machine, and, through the methods of esoteric prayer, comes into contact with the superhuman consciousnesses that inhabit the cosmos. The Voudon Gnostic climbs the cross and hangs on it just like Legbah-Osiris-Christ, and from there, in the twilight of time and space and life and death, he accesses heavens, hells, and all creation.

The Voudon Gnostic accesses his *syzygus*, his invisible twin. He molds the clay of creation with his own hands. He gives life with his breath and squirts magical poisons from his physical and ethereal sexual fluids.

4

Bertiaux and *The Voudon Gnostic Workbook*

The Voudon Gnostic Workbook (VGW) was not intended to be read from cover to cover and is not guided by a narrative thread. The workbook is a series of lessons that introduce the world to the vision of one Voudon Gnostic, Michael Bertiaux. First published in 1988, it soon became a hit within occult circles and was elevated to something of a cult status. Before that, part of the Voudon Gnostic system had already been briefly presented in some books by Kenneth Grant, such as *Cults of the Shadow* (1975), in which the author discussed Bertiaux and his system, considered by Grant to be innovative and very interesting.

It is evident that Bertiaux, in doing so, brings with him the whole sum of teachings the lineage he carries presents, from Jean-Maine and from the beginnings of the system as coined in Haiti. In this way, although Bertiaux presents everything through his particular perspective, we need to understand that the entire richness of the system is described there in the VGW. Thus, those interested in Voudon Gnosticism will necessarily have to dedicate themselves to the book, reading it and doing the suggested practices.

However, since VGW is not linear, you don't have to worry about starting on the first page and ending on the last one. The sections can be addressed independently and each in its own time. As passed to me by my initiator at OTOA, I suggest that the reader look at the sections that interest him the most and start with them. I would just add to this suggestion a simple idea: start, in fact, with lucky Hoodoo. The reason for this is far from mysterious. It seems to me that this is the most beginner-friendly section and also one that gives a good idea of how the system works, but we will discuss this further in a later section.

A popular opinion about VGW is that it is extremely complex. Certainly, all the nonlinearity inside of it contributes to this notion, but not only that. In fact, some terms, neologisms, and concepts that are worked on by Bertiaux can be challenging. In addition, constant references to strange places and realms, other dimensions, and magical machines are also often a common source of confusion.

The complexity of VGW never ends, but the difficulty in understanding it will dissipate as practice and studies progress. It is my wish that this small work that you are now reading will help you to face VGW as something more accessible, but even so, I cannot fail to emphasize again that it will take a lot of research, dedication, and conversations with spirits and visits to realms and dimensions in order for you to better grasp the book.

Among the many sections of the book—and the many arms of the Voudon Gnostic system—I highlight a few key chapters: "The Power of the Spirits," "Ghuedhe Grimoire," "The Genius of IFA," "Voudoo and Atlantean Research," "Zothyrian Metapsychology," "Gnostic Energies in Esoteric Hinduism," "The Erotic Magick of the Future Aeon," "The Shintotronic System of Gnostic Magick," "The Esoteric Roots of the Gnostic Power," and "The Gnosis of Spiritual Life." However, to understand exactly where all these chapters and many others came from, we can simply refer to the preface.

Prefaces are often ignored, which is not only a mistake but a shame. Keys for understanding the works are often given in these sections, either through some perspective or through some other information that will give the context in which they were produced. Bertiaux opens the preface to the VGW by stating that he will "tell us about the world of esoteric prayer from his own personal experience." This is the first big key revealed. Here, we are told that everything that follows is being passed on from the very personal point of view of the author. In other words, our point of view may be different.

Continuing in the preface, another great key is offered to us: all this work is based on contact with the spirits—Les Vudu. Esoteric prayer is then explained, and we learn that it is nothing more than conversations with spirits. For Bertiaux, this is the heart of gnosis.

Gnosis is a term that causes a lot of confusion. The most common translation equates it to knowledge. However, the rational idea of knowledge that we have in the contemporary world is extremely poor and unworthy of communicating what gnosis is indeed. Gnosis is an intimate knowledge that comes from experiences and that connects us to the invisible. Therefore, it is something very far from knowledge as we understand it today.

Thus, we can now say with certainty that *Voudon Gnosticism* is indeed an excellent term. After all, we are dealing with diverse, hybrid, and esoteric experiences that, mainly through the action of spirits or agents of the invisible, connect us to the invisible, to the divine, to the abstract.

We have already reached some very relevant points, and all that we have discussed so far, we have practically done just by looking at the preface. I'm sure you can already imagine the richness that is encoded in the more than six hundred pages of the VGW.

The other secret that we will learn throughout the text and the experience is that spirits—Les Vudu—are multiple and plastic. Endless and in infinite forms and ways. Thus, we are facing a series of lessons about contact with these beings that are beyond and "between" and immanent and that are able to teach us things, reveal secrets, and offer powers.

This question of the plasticity and multiplicity of Les Vudu is fundamental. This means that these entities comprise an endless myriad of experiences and subsystems within the Voudon Gnostic system. For example, we know that the spirits of the Voudon are the same as the Norse gods—this is just one side of their transformative ability. Indeed, these spirits can assume unimaginable forms.*

When we look at the book with these keys in mind, we begin to understand why it is a series of nonlinear lessons. In addition, it is easy to grasp that the spirits will be able to reveal particular and different information to each one, as well as provide unique experiences.

There is still much more that the VGW can reveal to us. As it would be absurd to try to reproduce here the teachings or insights contained in the said book, we can take a much more reasonable route and try to summarize some of the things that we can find in its pages. Of course, we will fail in the task of making a worthy summary, but if we succeed in arousing curiosity and the desire to know the book better, we will certainly have achieved a very beautiful objective. So, let's make a diverse and colorful overview of what can be found in this real grimoire!

LUCK SPELLS

A tour through the VGW will reveal methods and theories for very diverse things. For example, in the lucky Hoodoo chapter there are teachings regarding mind control and even spells to attract material gain. Now, despite all the discussion about esoteric prayers and spirits, let us not forget that we are living in the material world. This Hoodoo is, after all, lucky and, therefore, should be successful in many areas of life.

Hoodoo's luck, however, is not always so obvious. Tau Zendiq in his book *Keys to the Hoodoo Kingdom* reminds us that most of lucky

---

*I refer the reader to the book *Syzygy: Reflections on the Monastery of the Seven Rays* by Tau Palamas in order to see a manifestation of Les Vudu inspired by the Christian priests of the desert.

Hoodoo's lessons are concerned with providing tools for the operator to deal with customers. This is an interesting insight, though nothing prevents him from using those lessons for himself. However, Zendiq also highlights that the favors received by those who are immersed in lucky Hoodoo can be much more subtle than winning the lottery. We can put it this way: the spirits of Hoo and Doo will be like friends and help in surprising and often totally unnoticed ways. How and when this will happen will depend in part on the relationship between them and the operator and in a good part on the context.

So we need to get out of our minds the idea that lucky Hoodoo is a bunch of formulas for generating millionaires and Don Juans. The grimoire in question deals with materiality, yes, but always guided by the action of the spiritual world. Therefore, we must pay attention to the fact that the results will not always be exactly as we expect and try to understand this as part of an important exercise.

VOUDONIST CONTEMPLATION AND THE LINGAM OF THE DEAD

We discussed things like winning the lottery, but of course there are sections in the VGW that are devoted to more contemplative magical processes. Indeed, there are operations that will be challenging to those who do not have reasonable control of the astral world. For example, there are instructions and practices for the guidance of consciousness toward the building of astral temples. Symbols are ordered as the mind dictates, and thus machines or magical spaces are constructed. These techniques enable one to obtain definite results because of the strength derived from the symbols used.

Building an astral temple is a relatively common technique within the Western esoteric tradition. However, it is the uses that the astral temples of Les Hodeaux present in the VGW that are innovative. For example, there are hints of shape-shifting, with the wizard turning into an arachnid. As if that wasn't surprising enough, these temples can also be used for time travel. Of course, there are countless other possibilities for using these magical spaces. It will be up to the wizard to explore the potential of these sites and see what they can offer.

The priests of the astral shroud are referred to in the workbook as *les Linglesoux*, a name derived from *lingam* (Hindu phallic symbol of the god Shiva) and *le soi* (the self). Other practices, such as those revealed in the techniques of the les Linglesoux, allow the operator to become or, rather, to connect strongly to a spirit of the cult or family of Ghuedhe, who are lwas of death and have a strong connection with eroticism. The use of erotic power and sexual magic will be discussed in chapter 8, but for now, it is enough for us to understand that these are of frequent use in the Voudon Gnostic system and that these les Linglesoux techniques are considered equivalent to those revealed by the VIII° (eighth degree) of OTO.

This union of the Ghuedhe spirits with the priest or mage allows him to lodge these spirits within himself and awaken them, activating their powers. The ramifications of this are really wonderful, as the number of spirits is huge and the combination of awakened spirits can, for example, generate infinite possibilities for exploration.

VOUDONIST MAGIC CHAINS AND THE MAGIC CONSTRUCTION

Going beyond spirits derived from Haitian Vodou and magical practices of astral constructions, Bertiaux refers to Aiwaz in his workbook, which is obviously a derivation of Aiwass, known to be a pivotal figure in Thelema. The VGW connects Aiwaz to the Zothyrians who would have put him in charge of communicating the Thelemic current to the world. We discuss the Zothyrians later, in chapter 7, but in short, they are humanoids who inhabit an alternate universe structured by magic. It is important that we talk about the references to Thelema in the VGW, as it is not infrequent that some readers understand that the Voudon Gnostic system and the OTOA are Thelemic. In fact, this is a misconception.

What is being communicated in the VGW is that Thelema is a current, like the others, without any precedence or exclusivity.

Thus, what is clear is that the Thelemic current is one of the possible elements that can be used in the composition of the magical universe of the Voudon Gnostic system. However, there are so many places and so many landscapes to be visited and worked on within the Voudon Gnostic system that it is perfectly possible to spend a lifetime ignoring Thelema or any other specific stream and still do genuine work.

This notion mainly tells us that the pieces of the Voudon Gnostic system can be assembled in different configurations and that a student need not explore all the elements presented in the VGW or in the Monastery of the Seven Rays. This can lead to the false notion that the Voudon Gnostic system is an "anything goes" and "nothing is essential" system, but a careful reading of the VGW will show that there are several different ways of exploring the same themes and that everything is connected by the actions of Les Vudu.

Since we mentioned the issue of different configurations, we need to note that it is in the aforementioned Ghuedhe Grimoire that Bertiaux gives us another important key to the interpretation of the Voudon Gnostic system when he states that the magician does not waste the chances of building his own magical system. This means that everything VGW teaches must be used for this purpose. In other words, the VGW instructions are not like those typically found in the Western esoteric tradition, which must always be strictly followed and preserved. The VGW provides a base that must be used for new configurations.

It is within this magical system, which was passed on to and worked on by Bertiaux, that the apparently disparate elements of the VGW fit together because, as we have already noticed, they are part of a large network. Bertiaux discusses the I Ching, *ojas* (fundamental magical powers, which he calls "sexual radioactivity," that can be projected by the body in the form of rays), and even UFOs, which are definitely not the typical flying saucers but rather types of magical projections. He also discusses at length chakras, including the chakras of the gods who inhabit the cosmos. Although each discussion is independent, the dedicated student will realize that they are all connected by conducting wires, the biggest being, without a doubt, the construction of a magical reality of its own.

There are other fundamental points that connect them, such as spiritual interaction, which we have already discussed, and also sexual magic, which will still be analyzed in this work.

AFRO-ATLANTIC TRANSFORMATIONS

Other elements of African roots also emerge in VGW. This is the case with Fa, what Bertiaux refers to as the "Genius of IFA." Fa or Ifá is the name given to a divinatory system that consults or channels Orunmila, a deity of wisdom and knowledge. Ifá is also a philosophical system and a cult. Interestingly, Ifá divination or even Ifá worship does not seem to have reached Haiti, at least not in a similar way to what we see in Africa. Bertiaux, however, reveals to us that the esoteric Vodou system and also the Zothyrian system (remember, both are connected) work with the powers of Fa, which is nothing more than a fundamental magical force that created both Les Vudu and the sixteen monads, which find an evident relationship with the sixteen signs of Ifá.* We are, in fact, facing a system that is based on a fourfold division, the number four being, then, the fundamental number, from which we derive the sixteen signs. So we have a completely new Fa reading that is done from a clearly magical point of view, totally different and distant from traditional African worship.

Although the case of Ifá is truly emblematic, it is not difficult to notice how African and Afro-American concepts permeate the entire system of Voudon Gnosticism. Bertiaux justifies this throughout the VGW several times, stating categorically that all the lessons presented derive from the esoteric Voudon, which contrast with the exoteric Voudon or what we popularly know as Haitian Vodou.

---

*I recommend reading William Bascom's *Ifa Divination* (1991) and *Ifá: A Forest of Mystery* by Frisvold (2016).

This discussion requires care and sensitivity, as it is easy to see esoteric teachings as deeper and truer and exoteric teachings as more superficial and simplified. Such a viewpoint would certainly be a disservice to the complexity and beauty of Haitian Vodou and would further promote the oppression of this spirituality, which is already massive. Therefore, we must be clear: understanding the "exoteric versus esoteric" binomial from a quantitative point of view or ordering these elements in a hierarchy is a mistake. When we talk about exoteric and esoteric, we talk about dimensions that complement and talk to each other, each being suitable for a specific context.

VUDOTRONICS AND THE MAGIC CYBORGS

The Ifá-Fa outfit just discussed is certainly innovative, as are the constant references in the VGW to machines, engineering, and what Bertiaux calls the "science of Vudotronics." The esoteric engineering described in the VGW is unusual and interesting. It is through the occult engineering and construction of these astral machines, which have astral "parts" or "systems," that various magical operations can be successfully formulated. A simple example of an esoteric machine would be an altar, with a concrete component and an astral double that captures the more subtle forces. Through the altar, the mage can collect ethereal powers and concentrate them for his operations.

Thus, VGW's esoteric engineering looks nothing like the kind of bizarre science that would be characteristic of a comic book villain; rather, it is a collection of magical plans and schemes. The creation of Vudotronic machines can even take place inside the body, with designs that link the *points-chauds* (hot points), which are special power points on the body, to the invisible, transforming the magician into a true Vudotronic cyborg. Consciousness and spirit are the fundamental raw materials of this fantastic engineering, which sometimes is also programmed through magical computers.

VOUDONIST ALCHEMY AND ALTERNATE WORLDS

But, if we want, we can steer away from this somewhat futuristic engineering toward more familiar traditional places, such as alchemy, which also comes into play in the VGW, especially when discussing Legbah-Osiris and Legbah-Christ. Legbah is a spirit of the gateways and also related to crossroads, a mediator between the invisible and visible worlds, which we discuss further in chapter 9. Osiris and Christ are dead and resurrected entities found in the center of the cross, which is also the main point of the crossroads and in the "between worlds." As in the works of the Hermetic Order of the Golden Dawn, the figure of Osiris and his death and resurrection are closely connected to the dying and rebirth of the initiate, who passes through the alchemical phases of *nigredo*, *albedo*, and *rubedo*. Here, we again enter into a fourfold division, the basis of the Voudon Gnostic system, since the cross divides the plane into four quadrants. We are also talking about the four classical elements—earth, air, water, fire—and their role in the journey of the initiate.

Furthermore, the identification of the initiate with the figure of Legbah is one of the great mysteries of the Voudon Gnostic system, as it deals with the union nourished by Eros, by the erotic power. See color plate 3. Christ, Osiris, Legbah, and the logos structure energy. The erotic union with this combined structuring force triggers the elevation of the initiate. In fact, this union could easily be the subject of an entire book, such is its complexity and such are the possibilities triggered by it.

Throughout the VGW text and lessons, Bertiaux makes connections among Atlantis, Voudon, and Zothyria. He does this because the powers of Fa and Les Vudu were routinely worked out in Atlantis, and the magical Zothyrian Empire expanded these developments. Some question whether Atlantis and Zothyria actually existed and whether one must believe in their concrete existence. A key to answering this question is in the VGW itself. Bertiaux discusses "Zothyrian metapsychology," which suggests that we are within the realms of the metaphysical.

In this context, it is worth noting that Zothyria seems to be, therefore, an ontic realm or a realm of the imagination, a place that exists between universes and beyond space and time that fuels the power of the magician. Zothyria, like Atlantis, is a dimension of its own. In short, ontic in this context means something fundamental and with a very specific character. We explore this question further in chapter 7.

Eventually, the student and practitioner of the Voudon Gnostic system will receive communications from Les Vudu, and her own domains will reveal themselves and build themselves up. Such a construction will answer many of these questions, to which formulating an objective answer now would perhaps even be harmful.

Anyway, many other subjects are explored within the VGW, and as we have already warned, it is impossible to address them all. In later sections, we will discuss in greater detail some of the concepts discussed here, and we will present others that are also found in the lessons of the Voudon Gnostic system.

The reader who was not familiar with the VGW is now at least familiar with the character and spirit of this precious book. The next step, without a doubt, is to dedicate yourself to its study and begin to unveil all the teachings codified in its numerous pages. In the next chapter we discuss a little bit about the lucky Hoodoo.

5

Lucky Hoodoo

Lucky Hoodoo is the section of the VGW that I consider to be the best gateway or introduction to the Voudon Gnostic current. In addition to this section being simple and having easy practices, those practices are capable of initiating truly interesting experiences. Contact with spirits is well represented in this section of the VGW, as is the art of esoteric prayer.

My comments, in this chapter and the next, on this section in the VGW serve a dual purpose: to present and explain the material and also to reveal a more personal interpretation, which I hope, in addition to offering something new to those who are already familiar with the Voudon Gnostic system, will stimulate readers to return to this chapter after reading and practicing lucky Hoodoo. Just to be clear: the following discussion is my interpretation of the system in question.

Bertiaux traces the beginnings of Hoodoo to Atlantis. In the myth, Voudon was the religion of Atlantis. When the island sank, Atlantis was not destroyed, and its inhabitants, among whom were powerful wizards, were not killed. The inhabitants became powerful spirits with fish-like, frog-like, and snake-like bodies, and the island continues to exist at the bottom of the ocean. Bertiaux calls the transformed inhabitants of Atlantis "Hoo-Spirits."

Half the power of Hoodoo comes from this island and from the Atlantean mages of the past, the Hoo-Spirits. The other half comes from the realm of the dead itself. Nothing beats death: the energy of the spirits of the dead is very powerful, and they, of all spirits, best understand life. The wisdom and capacity for realization of these spirits are astounding. Bertiaux calls these spirits "Doo-Spirits."

What, then, is the true nature of Hoodoo spirits? Now, it seems clear to me that we have a play between magic and life. We must realize that the spirits of Doo, the spirits of the dead and death, are actually all about life. After all, life and death are inseparable aspects of the same thing. The secrets of one are revealed by the other and vice versa.

Magic is the most mysterious element of this equation. Though we are alive, we understand very little about life itself, truth be told, and we need to learn how to animate this magic to enchant our life and realize accomplishments. This will also help us to better grasp our very lives. That is what the spirits of Hoo and Doo accomplish. That's precisely the reason why life and magic always go hand in hand. Together, Hoo and Doo form Hoodoo, an amalgamation that means, in the end, *magical life*. This, in other words, could be described as an existence that is truthful and precious.

H. P. Lovecraft, an American writer of fantasy and horror, created a mythology of cosmicism, one of his most popular works being "The Call of Cthulhu." The island beneath the sea may be the abode in which Cthulhu, the leader of the spirits of the Hoo, sleeps. In fact, Cthulhu would apparently be pronounced Khlûl-Hloo—which seems to be a form or title for the great spirit of Hoo. Note the similarity between *hloo* and *hoo*. The relationship between reptilian and amphibian Hoo spirits and the "Great Old Ones" of Lovecraft's mythology is straightforward and has been explored by both Bertiaux and Kenneth Grant; in chapter 12, we delve further into Lovecraft's mythology.

The true meaning of *hloo* and *hoo* was evidently lost in translation. The passing of messages from nonhuman intelligences to mediums is not an exact science. Various filters exist, and information and sensations are often distorted. However, there are ways to regain these senses, and meditative exploration is one of them. Thus, we clearly point out to a linkage between Hoo and Lovecraft's Cthulhu myth. However, that's not all.

Hoo spirits' connection to the water element is not accidental. After all, water is the cradle of life. This means that the Hoo is also the seat of the magical origin of things. In other words, creation is Hoo's work. Therefore, Hoo is an integrative path and one of the two paths that forge the Hoodoo's magical journey. In this case, Hoodoo means the operator, the Hoodoo man.

As a path that promotes growth and creation, Hoo is represented by the transformation of Atlantean mages into aquatic creatures. Furthermore, the allegory of Cthulhu sleeping is evident. Therefore, we have in Hoo the potential energy to unfold or even all the innate capacities. Hoo is nature in all its expression and potential. However, Hoo lacks a significant element, which is renewal. The INRI (*Igne natura tenovatur integra*) formula teaches us that through fire nature is fully renewed.

The Hoo and Doo formula then reveals itself as an alchemical marriage of fire and water.* Therefore, Doo's spirits are allotted fire, and this makes sense, as fire is the ultimate tool of annihilation. Thus, it is by the flames of death and the ardor of the end that nature is renewed and transformed. The dynamism of fire enables nature to continue its journey of growth and transformation, just as death is the element that provides life. So there is no Hoo without Doo and vice versa.

Still, in the case of Doo, we have a probable digression of *doun* or *dou*, which in this case would connect with *om* or *oum*, the synthesis of reality or consciousness for the Hindi. Thus, *d-oum* would allude to the fact that consciousness is immortal and would seal the issue that Doo's spirits operate in a kind of *memento mori*. Furthermore, the association between fire and the soul is ancient.

---

*I am aware that Bertiaux attributed the direction of north and element of earth to the Doo spirits in the *VGW*. What I am presenting here is a fresh and different perspective. By no means am I implying that the original attribution is incorrect. The take I am proposing is just another layer of the same mystery. For this new interpretation I have taken inspiration from the Gede family of Haitian Vodou and also in fire/water and draught/ rain balance present in some Bantu cultures.

However, a third element remains to be added to Hoodoo—air. Kabbalist teachings reveal to us that air is the mediator between fire and water. Obviously, when we talk about air and its association with rationality, we are talking about the human element. Therefore, in this system, air is represented by the operator or by the sorcerer or shaman of Hoodoo.

Air, like humans, is ephemeral. This ephemerality is what links the air to the Hoo and to the Doo, for it is the birth and the dying that form the human journey. Air is also the fuel of vitality. Air is invisible, yet always present. Air is also the representation of life—often inaccessible, but always present and endless. So is death, unending and always around. Life and death are entwined again. Hoo is in Doo and vice versa, and air is the perfect mediator of that.

The last layer of the equation is, in fact, the earth, an element that is reached through materialization or concretization—that is, through the work of Hoo and Doo, which is performed by the operator. If we remember that the universe is a projection of the mind, not our own mind but the universal mind (*nous*), as Bertiaux teaches us, we will understand why the Lurianic Kabbalah school associates earth with the sphere at the feet of the Tree of Life or Malkuth. On the other hand, as materialization is the work of the master, the reason why Kether, the first and highest sephira, is in Malkuth, the tenth sephira, and Malkuth is in Kether is also explained. However, the Tree of Life is one of the more rudimentary symbols of the universe; the 231 gates of Kabbalah, created by pairing the twenty-two letters of the Hebrew alphabet, are a more complete symbol and one that comes closest to a diagram of the web of the universe, dominated by the twin brothers Anamse and Baron Zariguin. These two spirits represent the action of the universal mind in both sides of existence: being and non-being, life and death, universe A and universe B.*

---

*More about Anansi, the spider-spirit of whom Anamse is a manifestation, and the idea of it being a manifestation of the universal mind can be found in *Obeah: A Sorcerous Ossuary* by Frisvold (2013).

These four elements or points form the base that projects to a fifth point upward, which is the point of spirit. This point is the apex of the Hoodoo pyramid, which is also the representation of Legbah-Osiris, the point that protrudes from the meeting or the crossroads. This is the seat of the spirit, for it is here, in this middle, which represents the middle of a column or the poteau-mitan—which would be equivalent to the Tiphareth point on the Tree of Life—that the Hoodoo meets the spirits. So, more than a point of no return, this point is a state that can be reached several times.

Of course, this is a state that can be conquered as well. That is, if the Hoodoo sorcerer manages to fulfill his objective of achieving his magical life, of reenchanting his existence, he is in this state of mediation all the time. This does not mean that the Hoodoo will be in a continuous trance, but that she will be able to see the mechanisms and the subtleties and presence of the invisible in the visible; she will have acquired *le pris des yeaux* ("the prize of the eyes" or clairvoyance).

Thus, we have the representation of the pyramid with the eye at its apex, and its most hidden meaning is revealed to us.

Still, it is necessary to understand that the pyramid is the base on which the work of Hoodoo is based. Once the Hoodoo understands that it is the pyramid that needs to be built—that is, the understanding of the interaction of Hoo, Doo, person, and manifestation to reach the spirit—it is possible to create a system of work of his own.

6

The Atlantean Mages and the Immortal Hoodoo

Being an Atlantean mage and an immortal Hoodoo is part of what we are aiming to achieve as we walk the Hoodoo path. But what does that mean? We are pursuing a shamanic path that connects us to the invisible through Afro-Atlantean Voudon and Hoodoo techniques.

The beauty of these systems is that they are absolutely free of spatial-temporal constraints. This means that the spirits of Voudon Gnosticism and Hoodoo will present themselves to each person in a very different way. Consequently, the work guided by these spirits will not be identical either, although there will be structural similarities.

The spirits will teach the construction of spells and magical machines, with which the Hoodoo will work toward your achievements. Sometimes things can seem confusing. Keep in mind that this type of communication is not direct and not usually obvious, although it can be. Therefore, the Hoodoo needs to tune his magic antenna. The best way to do this is through simple exercises and the practice of Hoodoo rituals. We need to keep in mind that in magical traditions, developing relationships with the spirits requires work; the practitioner cannot simply follow formulas.

The lucky Hoodoo is thus a shaman, a mediator, and a wanderer whose noblest task is to make the invisible visible and bring magic to all aspects of life. The Hoodoo, however, has one foot in the visible and the other in the invisible, and in the end, everything will become the same for him. Therefore, the Hoodoo is necessarily someone unique, dedicated, and immersed in her magical work.

Anyone can become a Hoodoo. In fact, we are all already Hoodoos; we just need to understand that.* The first step in understanding that we are Hoodoos is wanting to become one. For this to be achieved, though, there is no escape; we need to work with the spirits.

Before we briefly discuss the spirits themselves, it is worth highlighting the meaning of "we are all Hoodoos"—this is not to say that anyone can do anything. What this statement highlights is that there are no special prerequisites or bloodlines or anything else specific for someone to become a Hoodoo. One just needs to have the will and do the work to achieve this goal.

Spirits are invisible and intangible but also very real forces that inhabit our universe. Trying to understand anything beyond this about their nature is to navigate mysterious waters. Many are frustrated because they think that spirits are not truly spirits but are rather just parts of the mind. Others, in turn, are sure that they are autonomous and conscious entities. The truth is, you can believe whatever you want, as spirits are not concerned with your understanding of them. They will still work with the Hoodoo and, little by little, will reveal more and more about their characteristics.

The first step on this journey is the ritual of dedication to the spirits of lucky Hoodoo, which is described in *The Voudon Gnostic Workbook*. I am aware that many people have problems working with spirits they are not familiar with. I understand, of course, this position. It's always good to understand what we're getting into. For this, I suggest thinking of approaching spirits as an approach of friendship. Dedicate yourself to them and be calm. If things don't go your way, for whatever reason, it will be possible to end the relationship without further damage.

---

*This is a running theme throughout Bertiaux's *Voudon Gnostic Workbook*.

Many people want to be absolutely sure about what they will gain from working with spirits, but they don't even know what they want or what they can offer. That kind of work is a two-way street. Are you really willing to dedicate yourself and listen to the spirits? Well, if not, don't expect results. Because it is a dynamic work that requires contributions from both sides, it is clear that we cannot view service to these spirits as servitude. Serving the Hoodoo spirits is more a work of self-dedication than anything else because a primary motivation of these spirits is to help the Hoodoo awaken to his magical life.

The awakened Hoodoo will become an Atlantean mage. In other words, she will remember the magic of Atlantis, where magical life reigned. This remembering, I believe, must be understood carefully—very carefully, I would say. We are not talking here about remembering things as we remember what we did yesterday or a few years ago. The memory of Atlantis is an impetus, perhaps a sensation, something that makes us live differently. It is the world's reenchantment mechanism. Remembering Atlantis is a step of no return, usually. However, it is not something static; it is dynamic and always present.

Nor is it as simple as turning a key in a lock. These are layers that are being overcome. The more you understand how to live your magical life, be a Hoodoo, and balance fire and water to make them earth with your air, the more the memory becomes clearer and more potent. The spirits of lucky Hoodoo and Voudoun Gnosticism will help. In fact, without the help of the spirits, this process, as I discuss here, is impossible.

That's why the Hoodoo is immortal. The moment the Hoodoo shaman begins to remember his Atlantis, he connects to the threads of the web of life and death and opens himself to a journey that will take countless lives. In the labyrinth that is constantly spun by Anamse-Zariguin, death and life are two sides of the same coin, revealing that there is no end to things, including ourselves. For color versions of the images on the facing page, see color plate 4 and plate 5.

Image 6.1. Spirits of Hoo and Doo. Photo by Eduardo Regis.

Image 6.2.
Hoodoo Wisdom.
Photo by Eduardo Regis.

7
Zothyria beyond the Stars: Inside Your Mind

I have already remarked that book prefaces and forewords are generally ignored. Other sections that are often ignored are those that appear at the end of the general body text. In the case of VGW there is a glossary that is often unknown. Truth be told, it's not easy to find it because of the colossal size of the book. But in this section of the book, there is an explanation of several typical terms that appear throughout the VGW. We are particularly interested here in the definition of Zothyria, which is identified as the name of an alternate universe, and that Zothyrian refers to all that within magic that is typical of the interest of the Gnostics. Zothyria is also an empire established in this distinct universe, which is completely structured by magic.

We're almost in science-fiction territory, some would say. Well, they wouldn't be completely wrong, but after all, we're dealing with magic, and without a little bit of fantastic stuff, what would our system be if not very uninteresting?

We have already discussed that the empire of Zothyria can be understood as one dimension of the many that make up a person's ontic sphere. This, of course, while not necessarily entirely subjective, can be abstract. After all, we know that the best state to access the ontic realm is between deep meditation and light sleep.[1] This is also the best state for programming magical computers, which will make logical connections among different Gnostic and magical realities. Well, this is how it is possible, therefore, to travel to alternate universes, such as the Zothyrian universe.

Be that as it may, it is a fact that Bertiaux has come into contact with Zothyrian intelligences several times, and in the VGW he describes the Zothyrians as humanoids that inhabit a distinct universe. What humanoids would these be exactly? Only communication through computers or other methods can reveal.

One of these methodologies is that of points-chauds, mentioned earlier, through defined methods and processes by which a system of thirty of these points is activated and allows travel to the empire in question. Certainly, there are others. There are even methods of contacting Zothyria that haven't yet been developed.

We are, however, getting ahead of ourselves. First, we need to better understand what this Zothyria thing is, as explained in the VGW. The planets, for example, are connected to Zothyrian magical forces, and their location, movements, and interactions are part of the expressions of these powerful magical forces of Zothyria. The Zothyrian Empire also contains, within its ranks, angelic forces and archangels. At one point, Bertiaux states that the Zothyrian elements are similar to the transcendental ego.

The concept of the transcendental ego is not simple, but I'll try to offer a reasonable explanation, navigating through Husserl and Kant (I'm going through some rough waters here, I know) with the help of David Carr and his 1970 article on these two philosophers, along with many others. The transcendental ego is a part of being that exists before anything can be perceived, felt, or known. It is unique to each of us and cannot be shared with others. Immediately, we realize that it exists but cannot be readily known—because, generally speaking, we only know or recognize ourselves through others. The transcendental ego is a fundamental, basic structure that is not revealed in a given way, and so within that deep mystery, it holds all possibilities. It is a kind of true consciousness, if you will. We could define it as the consciousness of all that is universal and real in a metaphysical sense and, because of that, unique.

Let's continue with discussing Zothyrian elements, and then we will return to the question of the transcendental ego. When discussing Fa, the VGW asserts that the Zothyrian system is similar, a kind of successor, to the esoteric Voudon of Haiti, as both are based on the Fa; however, they are not identical. Later in the VGW, Bertiaux states that the lwas act on the unconscious mind, while the Zothyrian demigods act on the superconscious mind, which is the part of the mind that we share with the divine mind.

Going further, we see that the Zothyrian Empire is essentially composed of the "pure form of the Gnostic logic of the ontic sphere" and that the Zothyrians are humanoid but not necessarily like us, as their culture is based on different premises. We are also told that the Zothyrian universe is "on the other side of Orion" in relation to the Nemironian system, of which, in fact, the Zothyrian Empire is an offshoot. In the VGW glossary we find that the Nemironians live on a planet in Orion and that, in some way, they are also in the minds of Michael Bertiaux and other initiates. Let us remember for now that Orion means "light" and that it is linked to the spirit.[2]

Following, we find that the unconscious mind and the superconscious mind become tools for the Nemironians and Zothyrians after certain processes of magical development. Not only that, but in the topology lessons we learn that all spaces of Zothyrian topology are within the magician's imagination and are arranged in his ontic sphere.

More information is given in the lessons on the alpha through lambda energies. Here, we have a surprising revelation—that magical energies can modify the bodies of Zothyrians in such a way as to make them dense like the human bodies, which they can then replace. Now, doesn't it look like we're discussing an internal change rather than an external change? However, appearances do not always point to the truth.

The discussion I want to raise now is one that is present in different fields of esotericism. The question is: Is Zothyria a concrete empire or is it a construction or layer of the mind, perhaps of the so-called transcendental ego? The answer is not easy, and probably, different readers will have different views about Zothyria. What I do know for sure is that discussing this doesn't change how the system works—and it does work! Therefore, some may think that we are just wasting words. This question is relevant, however, because we will be discussing the foundations of the entire Voudon Gnostic system. Focus is given on Zothyria, as this is, I believe, the most emblematic case for this question, among all that appear in the VGW. The answer I have to offer you is not an easy one. A simple "it is or it is not" is not enough.

One of the great lessons within the Voudon Gnostic system, which is presented in the Monastery of the Seven Rays, is that the "universe is a projection of the masters' minds." Let's ignore the masters for our present discussion and focus on mind projection. We could talk about the universal mind projection, but let's see what we can comprehend when we take a look at our own minds now. In fact, humanity has been debating the issues related to the subjective universe and the objective universe for a long time, in different ways and with the most disparate interpretations and points of view. Great thinkers have addressed this problem, and I, without any pretense of being on par with them, can only contribute one or two ideas.

Obviously, the objective universe is one that we can measure and know empirically. It is what we see, feel, and touch and what nature orchestrates. The subjective, in turn, is what is perceived and experienced by each person. The big question is: Is there a difference between them? At first it is tempting to say yes, but the more we think about this question, the more a simple yes may bother us.

We see, hear, feel, and touch everything through a series of physiological processes. For example, photoreceptors turn light into electrical signals, which travel to the brain. The brain translates them into images, which the mind interprets. Now, I don't mean to say that brain and mind are the same thing, but a connection between them seems indisputable. Even if we assume that mind and consciousness are not seated in the brain, we can imagine that they somehow work through the brain or are in control of it. Thus, the things we experience materially, through the senses, appear to be, at least on some level, also experienced in our mind or consciousness, which are also not necessarily the same thing. So, is it possible to totally remove subjectivity from any reality?

Without wanting to find a definitive answer to the question posed above, let's return to the Zothyrian Empire. We know that Bertiaux and others made contact with Zothyrian intelligences and that they instructed him in various concepts of the magical and Gnostic system that we know as Voudon Gnosticism. This does not provide any answers to the previous question raised, but let's keep this information in mind.

It is true that several elements in the VGW discourse on Zothyria point to processes of mind and spirit, such as metapsychology and topology, and even refer to Orion and its equivalence to spirit. On the other hand, there are categorical claims that Zothyrians are sentient beings from another universe. This question of the actual existence or not of Zothyrians is equivalent, arguably, to the notion of the Holy Guardian Angel (HGA), a kind of genius or higher self, so discussed in the Western esoteric tradition. Does the HGA exist externally or is it internal? Many have tried to answer this question and faced great difficulties.*

The answer to this question is twofold: Zothyria is both real and at the same time part of a mental projection that can be accessed collectively. Our society tends to classify everything on the astral plane as unreal; however, in the astral realms, in the midst of the ethereal, we find infinite universes that can be accessed by consciousness. So we can access and know Zothyria and establish contact with this empire and

---

*I am not implying that the HGA and Zothyrians are equivalent. I am just raising a point in order to help us think about the question in hand.

with these beings, who are humanoid in mind but not in body. This is precisely what Bertiaux is trying to communicate: there are entire universes inside us, but perhaps not literally "inside." It is necessary to give new meaning to the domains of consciousness and mind and to the idea of the universe. The nature of these universes exemplifies the Hermetic principle of "as above, so below."

The more the Voudon Gnostic understands this reality and masters this ability, the more her connection with Zothyria increases and the communication with the Zothyrians becomes more frequent. By this way, the Voudon Gnostic can pass special initiations that allow for the awakening of new powers and new perceptions. This is the way in which the Voudonist is becoming more and more Zothyrian and in which Zothyrians are also gaining a body of dense matter.

The body, by the way, which for the Voudon Gnostic is not in opposition to the mind, is part of this process. As the body, brain, mind, and consciousness are connected, the body is one of the keys to unlocking passages to certain more hidden mental and astral recesses. That's why we have techniques like points-chauds and why certain sexual magic techniques will be important for the Zothyrian connection and also with Les Vudu. Ultimately, the body and mind are both part of consciousness and are instruments for it.

Body and mind are the launching pads of the transuniversal buses that, operated by magic computers and Voodoo machines, make the connection between our universe and the Zothyrian or Z-Universe. To travel to Zothyria, you don't need more than the material we already have at our disposal, our mind and body; you just need to understand how to unveil, layer by layer, this mystery.

8

The Serpent and the Egg: Cosmic Sexual Magic

One of the bases of the Voudon Gnostic system is sexual magic. As noted in chapter 1, Lucien François Jean-Maine was versed in the mysteries of the OTO and the system of P. B. Randolph. Thus, we can trace, at least partially, the origin of the development of sex magic found in the Voudon Gnostic system.

It is clear, however, that we can go deeper into history to establish the relationships among love, sex, and magic. For example, the Italian scholar and Catholic priest Marsilio Ficino (1433–1499) said that magic derives all its power from eros. This notion of Ficino's is in tune somehow with what is brilliantly put by Ioan P. Couliano about the production of phantasms, a kind of artifice that the spirit manufactures from the sensations of the body and that would be readable by the soul, which would not understand the language of the body.[1] These phantasms, more subtle than words, would be images, and they would be fundamental to the art of memory, so valued by Giordano Bruno (1548–1600), the Italian philosopher who developed mnemonic techniques. In addition, erotic desire would be one of the most powerful ways to produce ghosts. In other words, eros would be a phantasmatic or imaginative process.

Interestingly, Couliano states that "magic is a phantasmatic process that uses the continuity of the individual *pneuma* with the universal *pneuma*."[2] Thus, he also firmly connects eros to magic, following Ficino, which in some way emulates the famous Hermetic axiom, "as above, so below."

Although the connection between eroticism and magic has long been known, sexual magic is still very misunderstood and much prejudice and opprobrium are directed at those who practice it. There are so many confusions that we need to be careful as we go forward. I do not mean to deny that there are magical practices that do involve the sexual act—which should, of course, be engaged only by willing and informed adults—but that is not the entirety of the sexual magic found in the system we are discussing. Furthermore, we should not see any problem in sexuality, and it is precisely because of our bad relationship with our own sexuality that sexual magic is a minefield.

When we speak of sexual magic in the present context, we are referring to encounter and union and also to erotic energies that can awaken very strong powers and sensations in humans. This sex magic is operatively constructed primarily on the basis of power points or points-chauds on the operator's body that can be awakened through erotic energy. These points are the bridge that allows Les Vudu to interact with the body. In addition, the very interaction with the spirits is an act of sexual magic, as it permits the union of two consciousnesses, a positive one (that of the spirit) and a negative one (that of the receiver)—or even of spirit and body, in the case of activation of points-chauds.

The act of uniting is very important in sexual magic, whether the union of two human consciousnesses or the union of human with Les Vudu; all kinds of unions pertain to this magic. Union of this kind is cosmic, a cosmic matchmaking personalized by syzygy. Syzygy is central to the philosophy of Valentinus (100–160 CE), a Gnostic Christian and important thinker who headed a philosophical school. In short, Valentinus formulated that syzygy, the pair, was necessary for the union that would lead to total completeness. This idea was central to his gnosis.

The Persian prophet Mani (216–274 BCE) is also important in understanding how the concept of syzygy is shaped in our time. This prophet was the founder of the religious movement known as Manichaeism, a term that today is full of mistaken and simplistic meanings. Mani believed that an absolute state of purity was the result of gnosis. This gnosis would be the knowledge that would make it possible to perceive the difference among the fundamental opposites of the universe, which would give an unparalleled clarity about its structure. Mani attributed his teachings to an entity he called Syzygus—his divine counterpart or twin. This entity bears a relationship to Socrates's daemon and to the HGA. We could also think here about our double in heaven, which conforms to what is stated in the Ifá creed.

In Voudon Gnosticism, syzygy appears again, as formulated by Valentinus, but we cannot lose sight of Manichaean thought. Our union with our own divine twin would be a key act in achieving knowledge of the pleroma, the total spiritual universe. This may very well be a way of achieving a state of pure and total gnosis, which is encoded in the Voudon Gnostic system. However, sexual magic goes further. I have already discussed briefly that the use of erotic energy—both sensory and mental—is one of the tools Voudon Gnostics have. Before giving some examples of how this energy can be directed for basically everything, it is necessary to take a moment to explore the question of the sexual magic of the body and mind.

In chapter 7, referring to the Zothyrian Empire, in which we took a journey through thoughts that permeate the entire Voudon Gnostic current, I stated that in this system the body and the mind are not seen as antagonists, which is not the same as saying they are essentially the same thing. It is necessary to recognize that the body and the mind or consciousness are working together and that they are intimately connected, but they have their own characteristics that need to be recognized in order to operate within their limitations and potential.

Sex magic can have physical, corporeal components, but it can also be performed through the consciousness or on astral planes. This is hardly surprising when we stop to consider how much sexual intercourse depends on the mind. Whoever thinks that sex is a mere meeting of bodies is terribly wrong because in the sexual act, whatever it may be, there are important exchanges between the partners that go far beyond the physiological processes.

However, sex does not require an exchange of energy with another person since it is possible to experience arousal and orgasm in a solitary way. Erotic energy can be moved in several ways, depending on the operator's preferences. How this is done really doesn't matter. What we are concerned about here is the flow of sexual force that carries enormous action potential. This is one of the ways, for example, of activating the previously mentioned points-chauds.

The activated and circulating sexual energy that is released during arousal and also during orgasm allows us, for example, to reach certain levels of consciousness that would be difficult to access under normal conditions.* These alterations in consciousness can be used for certain magical operations and for travel to infinite alternate universes. This release of energy can enable contact with nonhuman intelligences, and thus have an interesting oracular potential.

It is through the polarities that this mechanism finds its probable basis of functioning. Again, we're back to the syzygy idea. We want to promote a union, and for that, we need to define our objective. Whatever it is, once determined, we can use sexual energy to polarize ourselves oppositely and, just like in nature, these opposite charges will attract each other. This reminds us of P. B. Randolph and Maria de Naglowska when they write in their book *Magia Sexualis* that "Sexuality is the principle and fundamental force in all being, the force of the greatest power in nature, the most characteristic witness of the Deity."[3]

A quick and simple definition of sex magic is the union of opposite polarities, although this definition is far from complete. Please don't

---

*Some schools of sex magic believe that it is better not to release sexual energy through orgasm but to retain it as much as possible and accumulate it.

confuse polarities with biological sex. Both polarities are present in us. It is always important to point out: everyone is free to love and have sex with whomever they want and no type of couple is prevented from practicing sexual magic. We are here discussing other, more subtle layers. I understand that to the unsuspecting eyes, the discussion of polarities may sound limited, but I hope readers do not have that bias.

This is not to say that there are not certain sexual magic operations that will require sexual fluids specific to one sex or both sexes. In the VGW itself there is an indication of operations where the secreted "poisons" are used. These, however, are specific cases within the broad field of sexual magic, which, as I have already stated, encompasses possibilities for everyone.

I do not intend here to offer a manual on sexual magic, but it is important to mention that although everyone can practice this type of magic, not everyone will necessarily be prepared to do so. First, as with any type of magical technique, you need to have a base. Generally, this involves numerous exercises of visualization, breathing, astral control, and also body control. Without some degree of basic mastery in the most elementary techniques of magic, operations of any kind are unlikely to succeed. Also, it is particularly important to have maturity and responsibility when it comes to sex. Even in solitary techniques it is necessary to be aware of this, as some involve triggering arousal through erotic desire for someone other than one's partner or spouse. It is necessary to know how to set limits and deal with our fantasies, or sexual magic can be the source of a series of traps.

I go now beyond the Voudon Gnostic system for an interesting example of how powerful and versatile sex magic is. I do this because it is a very emblematic case and it involves a system that is widely known within the Western esoteric tradition. In his book *Winds of Wisdom*, David Shoemaker creates and successfully uses a method of sex magic to make voyages to Enochian Aethyrs by channeling erotic energy as a trigger of consciousness alteration, manipulating the polarities to reach the desired Aethyrs.

But we are discussing Voudon Gnosticism here, so let's go back to the points-chauds in order to state that there are brain centers and sexual centers of those points. The conjugation or union of the brain centers with the sexual centers awakens the spirits that inhabit these points and can cause different effects. The spirits that are in the sexual points are called daemons and those in the cerebral points, aeons. These spirits act in the body through sexual radiations and can also express themselves in fluids.

The union of polarities, the formation of pairs, is one of the constitutive bases for union with the pleroma. Upon attaining this completeness and this state of absolute gnosis, the human mind fully unites with the divine mind, and consciousness expands to reach all universes. Thus, there can be no doubt that, if we are working within a system (Voudon Gnosticism, for example) whose main objective is the construction of the magician's or Voudon Gnostic's own cosmogony, this gnosis through union is fundamental.

9
Legbah, the Lord of Sexual Magic

The god-man, the synthesis between the divine and the profane, is a mystery and a contradiction. It is not by accident or even some strange irony that the stories tell us that Christ was killed on a cross. The cross marks the point where everything is connected, and it is only at this conjunction of all things that a man who is not a man but a God could find his end and his beginning.

Ironically, Christ as a liminal figure and a transitional incarnation, instead of bringing us toward God, takes us further away from the divine. The reason is simple: because only Christ had this condition of being simultaneously divine and human, with an entire religion built in his name, we may feel that we are left at the opposite extreme, being essentially worldly and lacking the divine. The more powerful the God and also his intermediary, the more obvious our own limitations become. If we consider that God is an abstract concept and that the divine is a complicated mystery, few will be able to decipher it. From this is born a class of specialized people called priests. They supposedly know how to get closer to God and can tell us exactly how to do that. Instead of making us more familiar with the divine and the unseen, priests estrange us from it all.

Now let's think about early societies where the divine and God, or the gods and their intermediaries, were not so far apart. In fact, they were living in a dimension or an epoch (the so-called golden age, for example) in which the origin of everything was entangled with our world. Reality as we know it then would have been manifested by the will of the ancestors and the customs and laws they passed on. Every act in that dimension or time would have been an act for the divine—and almost every act here on this plane, as a repetition of the acts of the ancestors, would be divine as well.

Of course, there were priests; in some cases they were called shamans. These priests had a defined role and were able to do things that no other person could do. What they would not do, however, would be to regulate unseen wisdom or divine experience or interaction with gods and spirits. Customs did that, and everyone had to follow the same laws and conventions. Thus, in relation to this divine presence, everyone would be equal, even if different people had different roles to play in society.

We could argue that this traditional view of Christ is not correct and point out that Christ is not a person but a state of being. This point of view has already been the subject of many discussions, and I would say that identifying Christ as a state of being brings us closer to the divine because now the state of Christ can be attained by anyone.

I believe it is clear why a new perspective on Christ is needed. If we keep believing that Christ is unique, we are basically saying that we are doomed to live a life that prevents us from reaching our potential. When we assume that Christ is a stage to be reached or even that Christ is a means, then we have something we can use to increase our magical awareness and perception. In other words, Christ must be a tool to help a person become his own pope or, to be clearer, take control of his relationship with the unseen.

MR. NOON

The Voudon Gnostic system has a figure who can help you become your own high priest: Legbah or the Noon Master—the Christ of the Voudon Gnostic current.

Legbah is recognized as the Voudon Christ for very legitimate reasons. He is the mediator between humanity and the invisible, and he is a stage that can be reached—even if initially only for a brief moment. Legbah is the union: he is the son of the sun and the moon, and he has both polarities and therefore can act as a conduit from the visible to the invisible and vice versa. No one can reach the divine without Legbah.

Union is love, and the magical union of the visible with the invisible is Legbah's own role. Thus, Legbah is love, sex, sublimation, and condensation at the same time. He is said to be in the *midi* or in the center of existence. Legbah is the crossroads, the point where everything meets, blends, and takes on new colors and shapes. For this reason, he's considered a trickster and a cheater.

Legbah can become all at once and exists among the present, the past, and the future. He appears in many guises. In some he is stern; in others he is cheerful and can even be violent and really scary. Legbah is no Christ of Sunday Mass; he is the Christ of Voudon. Legbah not only makes our merging with the divine possible; he is even willing to help us if we know how to ask the right way.

By the example of Legbah-Luage we will be able to follow this thread of discussion. Luage, in a nutshell, was a priest who achieved union with Legbah. Looking at this case, we learn that the union of human with the divine is an act of sexual magic. Here, we see the theme of love versus strife as well (as Empedocles formulated). Love is an act of union that edifies, and strife is the conflict that separates. In sexual magic, we make use of these two concepts, which are contained within the idea of polarities. After all, there is no union possible without the concept of separation. So, to break the strife that separates us from the invisible and the divine, we need love, and the act of love is union.

It is also interesting to bring Valentinian Gnosticism into this discussion, as this is a case where syzygy's concept fits. Let's remember that syzygy is the pair and is about the union of the parts that make the whole. These parts are necessarily positive and negative. Here we see that the union of the visible and the invisible is an example of a kind of syzygy: the invisible, the spirits, Les Vudu will always be positive toward humans, while humans will be negative or receptive to the spirits.

Valentinian Gnosticism also tells us that this union is what brings about gnosis. Thus, Legbah is not just the one who opens the way in a literal sense, but also the one who opens eyes to the true world. This is why Legbah-Christ is central to the Voudon Gnostic system. Christ said that only through him can one reach the Father, and we see here that only through Legbah and union can gnosis be reached.

This union can present itself in numerous ways. For example, when in Haitian Vodou Papa Legba is asked to open the gates, we know that he is uniting the visible and the invisible and allowing things to merge and spirits to pass through. In a similar way, the Legbah of the Voudon Gnostic system is also a path opener because he can act as a bridge between the Voudon Gnostic's intention and the unseen and, as such, can be seen as the magical act itself. In other words, every act of magic would be an act of union, and in this we see why Legbah is a great magician and why sexual magic is the basis of manifestation.

10
The Magical-Spiritual Sessions of Hyde Park Lodge

In this chapter, I discuss and present to readers the method perhaps most used by Bertiaux to contact the invisible world of spirits and Les Vudu. It is a particularly simple method and precisely because of that extremely interesting. In the midst of this simplicity, however, there are layers, a powerful history of influences, and, above all, an unparalleled richness. What Bertiaux does is organic and extremely fluid. According to the *maître* himself, in an interview with Ariock Van de Voorde on Fulgur's website, this method was inspired by the spiritual work of Haitians.

It is evident that communication between human beings and disembodied entities—be they of any nature—goes back to ancient times. Since before written language, people have made contact with beings beyond materiality, whether through rituals, entheogens, or organic mediumship. As proof of this, we have Paleolithic cave paintings of shamans and other archaelogical evidence of ancient shamans and priests whose main job was to be mediators between the ordinary and the extraordinary in the form of spirits.

Evidently, over time and space, this contact took place in very different and particular ways. It would be quite a bold undertaking to attempt to discuss everything that has already been revealed on the subject; therefore, for the purposes of our discussion, it is sufficient that we focus specifically on more recent manifestations of this current, mainly from the spiritualism* that emerged in the nineteenth century, which although it was basically concerned with the contact between the living and the dead only, is of interest due to its proximity to contemporary times. Let's start this presentation with a little tour of séances in the modern world, so we can then pass to the next phase and remember what Haitian Vodou is like and move on to the Bertiaux method itself.

NINETEENTH-CENTURY SPIRITUALIST MOVEMENT

In order for us to understand a little bit about the spiritualist movement that emerged in the nineteenth century and lost force at the beginning of the twentieth century, we need to start with the Fox sisters (Leah, Margaretta, and Catherine) in the United States, in 1848, and their communication with spirits by raps.[1] See color plate 6. The sisters claimed that the spirits of the dead contacted them by knocking. The Fox sisters, by suggesting that the spirit world posssessed an astonishing materiality, took the nineteenth-century world by storm. Their contacts and visions eventually culminated in a kind of spiritual telegraphy, a method by which it was possible to make the spirits write sentences by tapping. This method of spiritual telegraphy had already reached England in 1852, through the hands of a Mrs. Hayden (Maria B. Hayden), an American medium who also brought to the Old World the first English periodical on spiritualism, *The Spirit World*, preceded by one in the United States, *The Spiritual Telegraph*.[2]

It was around this time that the medium Emma Frances Jay appeared in England.[3] She broke with the modus operandi of contacting spirits

*In English the term *spiritualism* is still in vogue, although Allan Kardec has pointed out that it is inadequate because all religions that believe in the survival of consciousness after the death of the physical body would be *spiritualist*. Because of that he coined the term *spiritism*.

through physical phenomena, such as raps and knocks. Instead, she went into a trance and while in that state managed to get in touch with the spirits. Obviously, contacting the spirit world through a trance state predated Jay, as we know from native peoples and the ancient world, but it was Jay who revived the subject in modern times, adding to the interest and fascination of making contact with discarnate or astral persons and entities.

Later, in the United States, the Davenport brothers (Ira and William) appeared and started what was called the "Spiritual Cabinet" (circa 1854), a show worthy of a stage magician, which impressed spectators with fantastic events, such as the apparition of "spiritual hands." The brothers were supposedly tied up and restricted throughout the apparitions, which would "guarantee" the veracity of the phenomena.[4] However, it didn't take long for it to be revealed that it was a sophisticated trick.[5] We could not forget to discuss the famous levitation of D. D. Home (1833–1886), another medium who was an expert showman. Indeed, a man levitating through action of the spirits must have been a show perhaps even more impressive than the Davenports' spectacle.[6] The Fox sisters were also eventually exposed as charlatans.

Table turning—gatherings of people around a table, brought together by a medium for contact with spirits, often accompanied by physical phenomena—became a popular pastime in Victorian England. The Victorian era yielded many curious pastimes, driven by a class with perhaps too much money, too much time, and not much to do. In addition to the parties at which the attractions were the spirits of the dead and the spectacular mediums, Victorian England also loved, for example, unrolling mummies from ancient Egypt.

It is true that many of these table-turning meetings were the product of a creative mind willing to exploit the credulity of others to gain some advantage, usually financial. In other words, many of these so-called mediums were charlatans. However, while it is necessary to recognize the presence of these deceivers, it would be imprudent to rule out that some of the mediums that emerged were, in fact, real, as it seems to have been the case of Florence Cook (1856–1904) and others, including many whose names are lost in history.[7]

One important figure in the world of spirits and people contacts was Allan Kardec (1804–1869), the pseudonym used by French professor Hippolyte Léon Denizard Rivail, known as the encoder of spiritism. See color plate 7. Kardec emerged as this figure with the publication of *The Spirits' Book* in 1857, which he wrote after being hit by the spiritualism wave that was spreading across Europe, meeting, in 1855, Madame de Plainemaison and being appointed by the spirit Zephyr as the herald of the dead. Kardec began to study the spiritual phenomenon incessantly and, taking advantage of his privileged education, was inspired by Mesmer's concepts of magnetism to formulate explanations about what he witnessed. In addition, Kardec conducted interviews with the spirits, extracting from them the answers to the questions he considered the most fundamental within the field. Kardec's method of interviewing different spirits—asking them the same questions and comparing the answers, with an almost scientific rigidity—seems to have been a great inspiration for Bertiaux and his companions. We will see that although Bertiaux and his cohorts were not concerned with determining the veracity of the phenomenon of contact between humans and disembodied entities, as they already assumed that it was real, they were certainly basing themselves on Kardec's "investigative" vein.

Another important character is Helena Petrovna Blavatsky (1831–1891), and she is particularly interesting to us because Bertiaux was heavily influenced by theosophy and the figure of Blavatsky. Before theosophy and her Tibetan-inspired Orientalist turn, Blavatsky toured the United States as a medium. Her career as a medium—and also in the Theosophical Society, truth be told—was attacked and she was accused of quackery.* Be that as it may, it is impossible to deny that

---

*More than a century after the attacks endured by Blavatsky, the specialist in forgery, Vernon Harrison, Ph.D., elaborated an accurate study about the charges that were made against her and concluded that she was innoccent. See Harrison's "H. P. Blavatsky and the SPR: An Examination of the Hodgson Report of 1885," theosophical.org.

Blavatsky, despite having renounced her spiritist past while still alive, was an interesting figure within this whole movement.[8]

All these aforementioned figures have influenced the West with their vision and way of understanding and connecting with the spiritual world. As I have already pointed out, although some, like the Fox sisters, the Davenport brothers, Blavatsky, and others, have been involved in accusations and confessions of quackery, their influence does not seem to have been undermined to the point of being negligible—quite the contrary. However, this is not the only axis we need to look at in order to understand Bertiaux's method. To this end, we need to return to the discussion on Haitian Vodou, which has been, so far, only introductory. Although it is not within the scope of this book to present a fuller explanation of Vodou, it is worthwhile to discuss some details a little more carefully now.

ORIGINS AND WORLDVIEW OF HAITIAN VODOU

Haitian Vodou arises from a complex process that began with the forced diaspora of a number of Africans of different ethnicities, primarily from Central Africa, who were enslaved and taken to the colony of Saint-Domingue. These enslaved people were fiercely exploited for their labor and subjected to and influenced by French Catholicism* and also French mysticism embedded in Freemasonry. From this cauldron of Catholicism mixed with the diverse religious beliefs of the enslaved Africans, different ways of interacting with the invisible world emerged over time in the colony. This is the genesis of what we now know as Haitian Vodou.

Understanding Haitian Vodou as a mere religion, in the Western sense, is a mistake. There is no clear separation between the everyday way of life and the spiritual world within the Vodou vision, which leads to this mixture within Haitian society itself. So, although many

---

*Although the Congolese already had contact with Christianity in Africa.

Haitians today are not Vodou adepts, the worldview that the visible and the invisible constantly interact is something that is within most of these people's constitutions. Perhaps it is from this notion of proximity and constant exchange between matter and spirit that the technologies that emerged in Haiti of contact between people and entities do not require much paraphernalia and codification. With this, I do not intend to classify Vodou as "simpler" than a Western religion. I don't believe in this vertical classification. What I want to clarify is that there is a more fluid and natural exchange between spirits and people. This fluidity, in conclusion, leads to more organic rites, and it also greatly enriches the interaction once contacts are established.

We do not find in Vodou, for example, cathedrals, clothing made of expensive fabrics, or gold-plated regalia. Vodou tools are natural, generously given by the land, and simple. The secret, after all, is not in these implements, but in how the conversation between this side and the other side of the mirror is conducted. Evidently, for an adequate and fruitful conversation to exist, both sides need to understand each other. For this reason, the lives of Vodou adepts are surrounded by these interactions, so that they share their existence with the invisible, enabling this affinity.

Vodou practitioners tend to experience spirituality in a way that is less ruled by generalizations and strict codes. Thus, creativity and spontaneity find space to emerge and develop. As a result, new ways of making Vodou—of interacting with the invisible—are emerging all the time. What will decide its validity is the authenticity of the connection with the spirits. From Vodou's strong sense of community, it is evident that certain customs and understandings are maintained in order for an identity to exist. However, in the individual interaction between a practitioner and spirit, the room for innovation is greater.

Therefore, when Bertiaux talks to Van de Voorde, in the aforementioned interview, and reports his fascination with the way Haitians use art to converse with the invisible, we can understand how Vodou aroused his passionate interest in this religious tradition. Being an artist himself—and we all can be artists—Bertiaux sees in those people a truth that he also recognizes in himself, and which he then allows to blossom.

HYDE PARK LODGE SESSIONS
AND *ONTOLOGICAL GRAFFITI*

Though we have been primarily discussing the VGW, to continue our discussion, I need to reference what is considered the greatest work of Bertiaux: *Ontological Graffiti*. In this huge book, full of surprises and mesmerizing paintings, Bertiaux provides us, in a clear and accessible way, with the keys to his method of contacting Les Vudu, and if I could call this method by any name, I would say that it is a "Voudon Gnostic spiritist session." It is now clear why it was necessary to first discuss the whole spiritualist movement of the nineteenth century, because, in a way, Bertiaux revived those times, promoting true magical spiritist sessions. However, as it could not be otherwise, the séances of Bertiaux and his group were not exactly identical to those of the spiritists of the past. In fact, if the ancient spiritists were aiming to speak to the spirits of the dead, Bertiaux and his companions were aiming at contacting a full range of spirit entities. Let's see how, precisely, these Voudon séances were conducted.

Before proceeding any further, a distinction needs to be made. The use of the word *medium* within the context of the spiritist sessions by Bertiaux and his group takes on new contours. While, popularly, when we talk about mediumship, we think of certain individuals who have special faculties, here we are discussing something slightly different. The medium within the Voudon Gnostic system is a magician, a mystic, someone who develops through exercises and techniques the ability to be a bridge. Therefore, if the reader does not have any *mediumship*, in the most traditional sense, he should not feel discouraged from moving forward in the practice of Voudon Gnosticism. We need, of course, to recognize that some people have a natural talent and greater facility for this type of connection with the spiritual and astral world, while others will find it more difficult. There are techniques, in this case, to allow a person to improve his skills in these fields. These doors are not closed to anyone. I repeat and emphasize: we are talking about mediumship in the context of Voudon Gnosticism alone. In the field of spiritualism and spiritism, the discussion is different and the conclusion is also different.

In the preface to *Ontological Graffiti*, Bertiaux tells us that "as mystics, we know for a fact of our inner selfhood that the Science Circle of Spiritism exists."[9] With this statement, Bertiaux presents himself to the reader as a living heir of the movement led by Florence Cook, Allan Kardec, and many others. After this statement there can be no doubt that his work is based on the lessons and phenomena produced by the spirits. For us this is very interesting, as it opens up the following possibility: because Voudon Gnosticism is a magical system based on interaction with entities, perhaps a spiritualist magic, we do not need to build all of our foundations in Western ceremonial magical systems. In fact, without this connection with the spirits, we will be far from what the Voudon Gnostic system purports to offer us. Therefore, we must not only free ourselves from the need to follow the more popular current of the occult, but we must also dedicate ourselves to cultivating the spiritualist vein within our magical practice.

As Nicholaj de Mattos Frisvold has already reminded us in his foreword to this book, Bertiaux is also an heir of Jules Doinel (1842–1902), to whom he attributes part of his spiritist methods based on the Gnostic Spiritist Church.[10] Doinel was the person who brought the Gnostic Christian Church back to life in 1890 in France, after some intense spiritual experiences. He was visited by Jesus and two Bogomil bishops and was made bishop himself by them during their visitations. After receiving the episcopate and the mission of "restoring Gnosticism," Doinel founded the Gnostic Church and passed on his episcopal lineage to several important figures such as Papus.

Considering this, we realize that Doinel is a perfect example of how the interaction between people and spirits is a powerful engine and how this contact is what legitimizes a spiritual work of authentic connection. In this sense, Bertiaux, when rescuing the memory of Doinel, does so to clearly establish that his concern lies in these legitimate and true contacts. This is one of the many clues that Bertiaux leaves throughout his book on how the system he organized and lives by is structured.

The séances conducted by Bertiaux and his colleagues at Chicago's Hyde Park Lodge between 1965 and 1975, which are the basis of what is revealed in *Ontological Graffiti*, clearly show us what this method of contact with the spiritual world was like. The description in the book of what they did is sufficient for us to understand their method, but the book still keeps details from the public eye, suggesting here and there components that were experimented with during the work of the lodge. The sessions usually involved contact with a supernatural entity through a connection with the spirit through the esoteric temple—that is, through astral contact—or through meditation on one of the entity's paintings, through a medium, who functioned as a *mean* of contact. In some cases, it was the contact through the astral temple that impelled Bertiaux to make a painting, which then became a communication portal and a meditation space for connecting with a spirit.

Although magical constructions, access to astral spaces, and contacts with spirits are not without a technical basis, Bertiaux's sessions were not as intricate as the ceremonies outlined by the Hermetic Order of the Golden Dawn by Crowley, Gardner, and other occultists of the Western esoteric tradition.* While the most traditional magical ceremonies are marked by a superstructure composed of microstructures full of precise steps and a certain performance rigidity as a way of turning the necessary keys and accumulating the required energy, Bertiaux's séances were and still are more fluid. In addition, the sessions benefited greatly from the assembly of a group of people who through the interaction of per-

---

*Here, I need to point out that this does not exclude their influence on the system studied here and that elements of these schools can be used.

sonal and sexual energies could generate more potency for the session and ensure a more fruitful interaction with the spirits. However, nothing prevents a spiritual contact, such as a séance similar to those outlined, from being conducted by a solitary practitioner. In any case, once contact was established with the entity, the participants began to question it and obtain answers, which were then recorded. This is the basic structure of what the séances run by the Hyde Park Lodge were like.

Please note that, in the previous paragraph, I have written about some of the teachings that Bertiaux only mentions very slightly in *Ontological Graffiti*. For example, the notion that séances were more fruitful when performed by a group that was exchanging certain energies. It is true that the notion that a group of people involved in occult work is capable of generating forces more powerful than just an individual is nothing new in magical practice. The concept of egregore is, without a doubt, the most popular in this sense, since it generally involves the sum of the forces of a group generating a kind of thought-form that is born from this union. In the case of the Hyde Park Lodge sessions, it is likely that the congregation of the forces present would build a bridge and a more palpable environment for the manifestation of an entity.

In addition, the way in which the construction of these combined forces took place is remarkable. Bertiaux points to the exchange of personal and sexual energies being used in the séances. Thus, we have a hint of what was going on in those sessions, but we don't have the exact details of how this was worked. If we remember chapter 8 of this book, we can understand that those techniques would be a powerful tool for those séances, including the use of points-chauds. Another possible way would be the donation of individual energies to the medium so that he could channel the spirit. As the members of the Hyde Park Lodge were quite curious and innovative, I am sure that the explorations in this direction were many, and I doubt that I would be able to exhaustively explore and discuss them.

Despite these limitations, we can continue exploring the methodology of these sessions. Though the answers given by the spirit during the séances were full of important knowledge, without a doubt, it was through his paintings that Bertiaux managed to establish his own way of representing the magical-spiritual experiences and also the hidden dimensions of the entities. The clear proof of this is in the very use of paintings as points of meditation and contact with the invisible world. We are talking about how certain images keep connections with Les Vudu and how these images connect to specific points in ourselves and trigger processes or interactions that manage to lead our mind and our own spirit to an encounter with the invisible.

As Bertiaux tells us in *Ontological Graffiti*, Hector Jean-Maine believed that ritual signs and symbols activated the psyche, allowing the passage among its layers.[11] Ultimately, what this will trigger will be a journey through the medium's reality and a legitimate contact with different types of spirits that are interspersed within these layers of reality, often hidden or inaccessible by other methods. This notion explained by Hector was made into a method by the Hyde Park group. In this method, they would conduct a séance by making associations triggered by images and using this process to unlock keys in order to make way for the spirits to manifest.

In fact, throughout Bertiaux's descriptions in *Ontological Graffiti*, it is easy to see that there was a lot of search for innovations in the methods of the sessions. For example, in one passage, Bertiaux reveals the use of magic mirrors as receivers of spiritual messages. We can only guess what other resources were used, but I know from Frater Selwanga's personal accounts that Bertiaux still uses a crystal ball in many of his works. Indeed, this open and fluid nature of the Hyde Park group sessions is entirely mirrored in the nature of the OTOA and LCN initiatory work. After all, they were a group of mages gathered and working as if they were in a big laboratory.

We are facing, for certain, a method of magical-spiritual communication guided by the construction of links and passages. If we look again at the study of the VGW with these eyes, we will notice that much of what is suggested and described there is either within this field or is building foundations for us to work on these connections. So, we see how the lucky Hoodoo's initial ritual, connecting us to the spirits of Hoo and Doo, makes perfect sense within this logic. These, after all, are spirits that will help us enormously in building these links.

However, more than just understanding the method of Bertiaux and of the Hyde Park Lodge in a rational way, as a mere technique, we need to think a little bit further. For that we also need to go back to our discussion on Haitian Vodou and remember that this fluid and constant communication with the invisible becomes a way of living life itself. The construction of a magical life and of an enchanted reality ends up being the final destination of any discussion within the great Voudon Gnostic theme, but perhaps it is while studying those séances that we can understand more clearly how this can only be accomplished by living with the invisible.

In one of the techniques described in the VGW, Bertiaux shows us a way to get in touch with Lucien François Jean-Maine, the bishop of Voudon. In light of everything we've discussed here, it seems that Bertiaux has generously provided an important technique for anyone who has the ability to comprehend it. Mimicking the experience of Doinel, Bertiaux's technique enables us to connect with the bishop, and along with him we have the presence of Legbah, the Christ of Voudon. Through the channeling of Jean-Maine, Bertiaux, and Legbah, we are ourselves at that moment bathed in a spiritual influx that legitimizes us and encourages us to continue our work. From this experience, though we may not notice it, we emerge transformed and better prepared for the work ahead.

Likely, some readers will find this whole discussion very different from what is normally found in books on magic within the Western esoteric tradition. Some will be strangely drawn to this prospect while others will reject it. I know that the strong spiritualist heritage of the Voudon Gnostic system is controversial, less than the Voudon element, for sure, but still controversial enough in a field dominated by a rationalist and technical view of Hermeticism. Here, where spirits meet our

Image 10.1. Jules Doinel.
Photo by unknown photographer.

spirit, a whole new system is born—as if triggered by the explosion of a star—fertilized by creativity, experience, and spontaneity. Feeling spiritual contact will also make us recognize ourselves as spirits, and thus we will be able to understand our reflection in the mirror in a more organic way.

Plate 1. A Vodou ceremony in Port-au-Prince, Haiti. Although the Voudon Gnostic system presents similar themes, these typical manifestations of Haiti are not part of this system. Photos by Fritz Rudolf Loewa.

Plate 2. A Vodou ceremony in Jacmel, Haiti. Note the color and the communal character. Photo by Doron.

Plate 3. Legba, the vodun from Benin, is a spirit related to sex, as seen by the erect phallus. When Legba reached Haiti and became Papa Legba, represented as an old man who limps, his sexual characteristics were diminished, but not completely lost. His cane can be seen as a phallus and is related to the *poteau-mitan*, or central post of the Vodou temple. In Voudon Gnosticism we rekindle the association of Legbah and sex. Photo by Jeremy Burgin.

Plate 4. Spirits of Hoo and Doo. Photo by Eduardo Regis.

Plate 5. Hoodoo Wisdom.
Photo by Eduardo Regis.

Plate 6. The Fox Sisters (from left to right: Margaretta, Catherine, and Leah) were pioneers in communicating with the spirit world. Reproduction of a Currier and Ives print.

Plate 7. Allan Kardec, the renowned systematizer who codified Spiritism as we know it today. Portrait by Antonio Bunarassi.

Plate 8. The Tree of Life with each sephira in the color it emanates in the realm of Briah. Note the correspondences with the human body. Image by Alan James Garner.

Plate 9. Bawon Zariguin. Photo by Eduardo Regis. This painting was previously reproduced in the anthology *Tumzantorum*, vol. 1 (Zoshouse, 2021).

Plate 10. A guia for the Doo spirits.
Photo by Eduardo Regis.

Plate 11. The guia for the Doo spirits shown from another angle. Photo by Eduardo Regis.

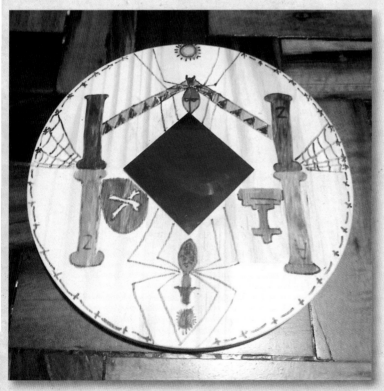

Plate 12. An example of altar that can be transported and hold candles and other objects. Note that it does not have to be fancy, nor do you have to be an artist to make one. It is only important that you create it with your soul. Photo by Eduardo Regis.

Plate 13. A small wooden box before being turned into an atua.
Photo by Eduardo Regis.

Plate 14. The atua after the process of painting and consecration.
This one is clearly Hindi-inspired. Remember: Les Vudu can take many masks.
Photo by Eduardo Regis.

11
The Voudonist Kabbalah:
The Gnostic Portal
of Baron Lundi

This work would not be complete without a discussion of Kabbalah. It really seems inevitable that we talk about it when discussing any movement or system within the Western esoteric tradition. In fact, from Marsilio Ficino (1433–1499) and Pico della Mirandola (1463–1494) until now, the Kabbalah has been intermingling with Western esotericism in amazing ways.

However, those of you who have already reached this point and have gone through the previous chapters certainly expect that the Voudon Gnostic Kabbalah will have some surprises in store. Well, stay calm. You will not be disappointed. This does not mean, of course, that the more usual mystical Kabbalah does not have its space or importance. We just deal with all these notions in a very specific way within the Voudon Gnostic current.

For this reason, we will not discuss here the basic things, such as the structure of the Tree of Life, the worlds, and everything that you will find in any text on the subject. We will jump directly to more specific issues.

This chapter will proceed on the assumption that readers are minimally familiar with mystical, Hermetic, or magical Kabbalah. See color plate 8. In case you need an introduction to the subject, I recommend the following books: *Mystical Qabalah* by Dion Fortune (2022), *The Chicken Qabalah* by Lon Milo Duquette (2001), and *The Qabalistic Tarot Book* by Robert Wang (2017).

Our discussion here will focus on the figure of Choronzon. The monstrous Choronzon, described by Edward Kelley as a demon of great power, is associated, in the Voudon Gnostic current, with Baron Lundi. He is considered the master of Meonite secrets and one of the pivotal Les Vudu in the journey of the Voudon Gnostic.

From his throne in Daath, Baron Lundi rules the passage from the universe of being to the universe of nonbeing. The universe of nonbeing, the great nothingness, and the great beyond is located at the back of the Tree of Life. Only through certain magical operations and certain secrets can the Voudon Gnostic open the gates of Daath and cross into this universe beyond the cosmos, beyond creation, and beyond all that can be named and thought.

This universe of nonbeing, the B-Universe or Meon, is a great source of magical power, as I mentioned briefly in chapter 3. Therefore, many mages and beings incessantly seek the keys to the gates of Daath, in an attempt to access the backside of the Tree of Life.* They try to decipher Baron Lundi's mystery and gain his secrets, but this is not a feat that many can accomplish.

If getting the keys to cross the Daath gate is not an easy task, imagine what comes next. We know that the journey up the Tree of Life from Malkuth to Kether, taking the upward path, is challenging. So what could we say about the idea of going down the middle pillar, all the way to Malkuth?

Traveling through the domains of the *qliphoth*, the evil forces, is certainly not simple. There are pages and pages written about this, so I

---

*Kenneth Grant discusses this at length in *Cults of Shadow* (1975).

don't need to comment on the subject at length. The fact is that the mage needs to know how to travel these paths or else he shouldn't even try to venture out. One of the prerequisites for having any chance of success is mastery of shape-shifting techniques. Still, the dangers are many, and it's easy to get lost. The fate of those who fail these journeys is obviously dire.

To pass through Daath and fall on the other side, conquer the ways of the qliphoth, and return is rebirth in the strictest sense. The passage to ineffable nothingness is like a return to the period of preexistence itself. The return to the A-Universe, the universe of being, is also a rebirth. Which brings us to the question: What exactly happens to these Meon newborns, godsons of Choronzon? Considering that the abyss, where Daath is located, was understood by Crowley and the Hermetic Order of the Golden Dawn as the manifestation of the Fall of man, we can then begin to guess what happens on this Kabbalistic Voudonist journey. By this more usual Kabbalistic view, Choronzon or our Baron Lundi would be a maintainer of humanity in its state of Fall, of disgrace. His main role would be to perpetuate humanity's separation from its divine state.

In Voudonist Kabbalah, we are interested in delving deep into Daath and going through Baron Lundi's mysterious initiatory rites in his Meonite temple on Uranus. Daath is not a mere adversary to be conquered; he is a guardian of treasures known only to Voudon Gnostics.

In this sense, the abyss, which is never irrelevant or even nontransforming in previous systems, gains new contours here and starts to be explored under a new perspective. This may seem like a footnote within all possible Kabbalistic explorations, but I assure you it is not.

The Tree of Life is the most famous Kabbalistic symbol. I know I slightly sneered at it in the lucky Hoodoo chapter, claiming there are better maps, but that doesn't mean it is worthless. The Tree of Life provides a pathway for interesting and complex explorations. As a cartographic representation of consciousness and the universe, the Tree of Life enables us to understand how to effectively traverse these territories.

In the case of the deep exploration of Daath and the backside of the Tree of Life, we find that we are delving deep into the Fall of man.

Some readers may be annoyed that we are now exploring Christian concepts but ignoring Christianity's strong influence on Western magic is a mistake. We need to ask ourselves if there is any interpretation of the Fall that can justify ignoring Christianity.

Let us turn to the Gnostic movements through the academic writings of J. Zandee. In general, the Gnostics understood that humans are the creation of the Demiurge, Jaldabaoth, as he is sometimes called. The Demiurge would be a mere imitation of the true and superior creator God and, as such, would be imperfect. Therefore, his creation—humanity—would already have been born in the bosom of imperfection. This Demiurge placed humanity in Eden, but in the Gnostic version, Eden is a prison, not paradise, and is an impediment to accessing true potential and knowledge. Thus, the Gnostics regarded the Tree of the Knowledge of Good and Evil as the very path to gnosis.

In the traditional Christian myth, we know well who tempted Eve to eat the forbidden fruit: the serpent, which would later be identified with Lucifer. But for the Gnostics it wasn't the serpent that led Adam and Eve to eat the fruit but Epinoia, a light that already dwelt within them and that Jaldabaoth tried to steal.

In Hebrew, the numerical value of serpent (Nahash) and messiah (Meshiach) is the same: 358. This suggests the two terms have an intimate connection or even express the same essence. The messiah is the serpent, which, in essence, is the fruit of the forbidden tree.

We are already equipped with enough elements to formulate some ideas about the mysteries of Baron Lundi. First of all, if we subscribe to the Gnostic view, the Fall might not have been such a bad thing after all. In this context, only through the knowledge brought by the light were we able to free ourselves from illusions.

Darkness covered the face of the deep, and the Spirit of God moved over the face of the waters.

God said, "Let there be light," and there was light.

It is at the bottom of the abyss, in the darkness of nothingness and nonbeing, that light shines for the first time. That's where we go after our innermost secrets. How to make this light shine in the absolute darkness of the unmanifest? It is not by accident that we are talking about Baron Lundi. *Lundi* is the French word for Monday—moon-day. The French word itself derives from the *lunae dies*, which means "day of the moon." The moon is the largest point of light in the night and symbolizes the light that will guide us through the labyrinth. We clearly see in Baron Lundi–Choronzon a Luciferian figure, who from a more traditional Christian view is considered an enemy.

Frisvold, in his exceptional book *Invisible Fire*, brings us Pasqually's view of the Fall in a very elegant way. Frisvold explains that Pasqually saw Adam as a priest-king and that he was placed in Eden, at the "center of everything," to maintain divine harmony on Earth. Thus, Pasqually would see the Fall as a departure, in fact, of humanity from living with the divine. However, Frisvold highlights that there is a secret in the Fall and in the consumption of the fruit of the Tree of the Knowledge of Good and Evil: to know evil and to be able to choose not to exercise it, thus establishing a glorious attitude and a notion of unity with the divine. Evidently, there is a close relationship between this evil and materialism.

It's clear that Pasqually's ideas don't mesh perfectly with general Gnostic thinking, but whether we choose to follow one or the other, we see that there's a recurring theme: the Fall is not mere disgrace; it carries lessons that can be converted into fundamental powers for gnosis.

This is one of the reasons why the Voudon Gnostic will delve into Daath to seek those keys that will be valuable in the Gnostic quest itself. The exploration of the Tree of Life, as it was configured after the Fall, is carried out to the last consequences in this context, all for the sake of a pulsating experience of the divine mind.

Voudonist Kabbalah is therefore a project of the cosmos and reveals to its dedicated student the points of interest and power that can be explored. In the work of building his own subjective universe, the Voudon Gnostic drinks from the source of these experiences to take control of this process for himself.

12

Necronomiconomania: Fear and Fascination beyond Yuggoth

One of the most outstanding points within the Voudon Gnostic current is the recognition that Howard Phillips Lovecraft (1890–1937), in addition to being a talented writer, was a living antenna for Meonite messages transmitted beyond Yuggoth. These were transplutonian messages that, in the midst of their aeonic radiations, brought images and teachings of the Great Old Ones.

Lovecraft, an avowed skeptic, never believed that his tales were anything but fiction. In reality, Lovecraft's opinion of himself and his work is not so decisive. There are things we express that are bigger than ourselves, whether we recognize it or not!

While alive, Lovecraft did not achieve fame as an author. In fact, he was a complete unknown, and his literary works were harshly criticized. However, his work was rediscovered after his death and came to be so celebrated that it has become ingrained in pop culture and is one of the best-known and most-explored fictional universes.

Lovecraft's writings are currently classified as cosmic horror. Horror is a genre that needs no introduction. It is the "cosmic" of this classification that tells us more exactly what he was writing about. In general, his short story "The Call of Cthulhu" expresses the idea that we human

Image 12.1. H. P. Lovecraft, July 11, 1931. Photo by unknown photographer.

beings are absolutely pathetic, irrelevant, disposable, and helpless in the face of the vastness of elements, creatures, and scope of the universe.

Nothing represents this idea better than the creatures that inhabit Lovecraft's tales and novels. From cosmic beings that inhabit our planet and that were once worshipped as gods to creatures from unknown places in space, all are very powerful and horrendous.

Arguably Lovecraft's most famous creation is Cthulhu, one of the Great Old Ones. This ancestral being, according to the stories, would be asleep somewhere in the Pacific Ocean, in the city of R'lyeh. It is wrong, however, to think that in his sleep, he would be completely forgotten. Cults around the world would try in every way to awaken him in exchange for promises of powers.

Another element that appeared in Lovecraft's stories and fascinated readers is the Necronomicon, a fictional grimoire that Lovecraft referred to in his stories, with a purported original title of Kitab al-Azif. Lovecraft created a fictional author of this sinister grimoire, a "mad Arab" by the name of Abdul Alhazred. Many believed it to be a real work, and people from all over the world searched for it in libraries and bookstores.

Image 12.2. Illustrations by Hannes Bok. Source: H. P. Lovecraft, "The Shadow over Innsmouth," *Weird Tales Magazine* (January 1932).

Many other bizarre creatures, races, planets, and objects populated Lovecraft's mind and were expressed by his pen. We will not make an inventory of his works and his universe here, as others have already done. What interests us more is to understand Lovecraft's connection with magic.

As I have already written, Lovecraft declared himself a skeptic and atheist. We know of his position from the content of letters written by him. There are a number of people, however, who insist that Lovecraft would have made these statements to protect himself from exposition, but there doesn't seem to be any strong arguments to support this hypothesis. What is documented, on the other hand, is that the author received certain inspirations through dreams, as was the case with Necronomicon, the name of his made-up grimoire. This is also sometimes used as proof that he communicated with nonhuman intelligences.

Without wanting to get tied down to any theory and certain knowing that we don't need to explain exactly what was going on in Lovecraft's head, I believe we can focus the discussion on the influence of his writings on magic. I've already advocated here that often looking for exact answers doesn't always change the functionality of things in magic. Let's keep that in mind. Only when we have already advanced in this discussion will I feel free to leave my interpretation about this theory.

It was Kenneth Grant who first began to significantly incorporate Lovecraft into Western magic. Grant brings Lovecraft's creatures into his magical system, understanding that they were, in fact, space intelligences influencing life on Earth. This notion espoused by Grant gained some supporters but also many detractors. Even today, Grant's adherence to the myth of Cthulhu is frequently discussed and criticized. Many contemporary occultists find his efforts to incorporate Lovecraft's mythology absurd or laughable. My honest opinion about those who denigrate the use of Lovecraft in magic is that they lack a clear understanding of how magic works and its nature. More recently, Phil Hine's *Pseudonomicon* (2009) further established Lovecraft as a source of magical tools and concepts. This book is entirely devoted to magical practices based on the Lovecraftian fictional universe.

Before Hine, however, another influential occultist who incorporated Lovecraft into his system was Michael Bertiaux. The Voudon Gnostic system and the VGW make references to Lovecraft's work, placing these entities and his fictional grimoire, the Necronomicon, as palpable elements within magic. Although Bertiaux did not give them the leading role that Hine would later give them in his aforementioned book, Lovecraftian creations are an important part of the great soup that makes up the Voudon Gnostic system.

One of the most frequent Lovecraftian elements in the VGW text is Yuggoth. Bertiaux equates Yuggoth with Pluto, as do others. He makes this equation because Lovecraft locates Yuggoth on the outer limits of our solar system, in the Kuiper belt. In the Cthulhu mythos, Yuggoth is home to alien races and cities. Although we have no evidence of any races or established cities on Pluto, we must remember that ordinary measurement and observation methods are not able to capture subtler emanations or emanations located in alternate universes. So let's not rule out any possibility!

For Bertiaux, the concept of the trans-Yuggothian would be connected to the idea of a space or an existence beyond the known, beyond what we humans can understand. Pluto or Yuggoth is also associated with Kether on the Tree of Life, which would suggest that the trans-Yuggothian is actually beyond Kether, either in the three veils of negativity or at the back of the Tree of Life. All these ideas point to the notion of things that are unknown, nameless, ineffable, and therefore potentially terrifying. Here we come closer to the Lovecraftian "cosmic horror."

This fear of something powerful and unknown is not exactly a new feeling within civilization. We need to remember Rudolf Otto (1869–1937), a German theologian and philosopher who was concerned with understanding the feelings that we mortals have about the divine. Otto claimed that when the divine confronts us, we surrender to irrationality, which triggers the notion that the divine can never be explained or really understood. In this way, Otto understood that we experience the divine through feeling. One aspect of this feeling that Otto highlights is *majestas*. Simply put, majestas is the overwhelming feeling of inferiority that we experience in the presence of the divinity, in all its power and in all our inability to understand it. In addition to majestas, Otto lists *tremendum*, which is the fear that the divinity arouses. It is not difficult to see that majestas and tremendum go together. However, Otto reminds us that the things that cause fear and confusion also attract us in strange ways, and so we also feel fascination at the approach of the deity.

This discussion about Otto's thought tells us that Lovecraft's "cosmic horror" and trans-Yuggothian radiations and beings, as well as Meonite aspects, have something in common, which is the ability to arouse these feelings, just as the divine does. The entire Lovecraftian mythology, far from being displaced within a magical-religious context, is well positioned. It is not surprising, therefore, that skilled and innovative occultists who perceived in Lovecraft's mythology the symbolic spark of an unquestionable truth welcomed Lovecraftian elements. In this scenario, the Necronomicon emerges not as a mere spell compiler, but as a revealer of mysteries, a holy book, a trans-Yuggothian bible. Therefore, this book, though it never actually existed, was able to arouse so much interest and generated a search for its "original" version. Several books with the title Necronomicon were published after Lovecraft's death, but of course these are constructions based on Lovecraft and not the supposed "true" tome. By this, I don't mean that these versions are not valuable, but we need to recognize them for what they really are.

Since there is no real Necronomicon, at least not as Lovecraft described it, the cosmic mysteries he described were left without a home

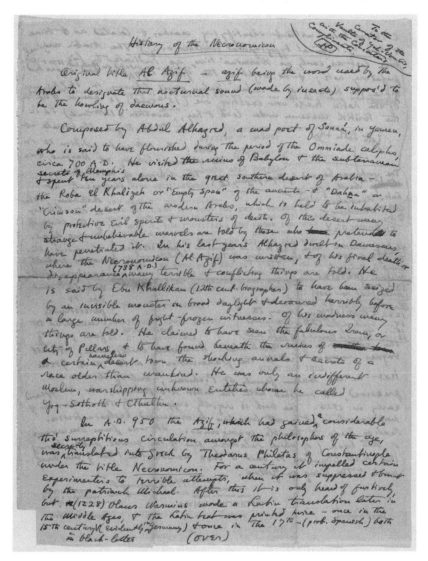

Image 12.3. Manuscript written by H. P. Lovecraft containing the history of the Necronomicon. Source: Wikimedia Commons.

to express themselves in spiritual and magical ways. Needing a space to be developed, I have no doubt that these symbols emitted attractive waves and called to themselves minds harmonized with their representations. In this context, the insertion of Lovecraftian things into the work of Grant, Bertiaux, Hine, and others arises.

So, the search for the Necronomicon proves to be a perhaps unnecessary effort, since multiple Necronomicons are present and others will still emerge. The Voudon Gnostic system embraces its version of the Necronomicon as one of the expressions of the universe and of the mind of the masters.

13

An Arachnid Journey to the Center of the Web of Worlds

Before entering the final part of this work, in which I will talk about OTOA-LCN orders and give simple and very quick examples of how to contact Les Vudu (all based on teachings described by the VGW), I received a communication from them that I should describe a particular experience I had with Baron or Bawon Zariguin.

This chapter will be different in style from the others because, according to the instructions I received from Les Vudu, it must be written like a short story so that the reader can follow the experience in a lighter way. According to my understanding of Les Vudu's instructions, this narrative will be able to activate certain cerebral and astral centers in the readers and stimulate the emission of electrophysiological Voodoo rays that will begin to produce specific Atlantean hormones that, through circulation via blood and transmission of magical-chemical signals, will cause subtle transformations that will allow a better understanding of certain Zothyrian keys encoded in the Voudon Gnostic system.

Without further ado, let's get to the story.

On one of those afternoons typical of contemporary life, in which work has already exhausted all our patience and in which the spirit is feeling particularly at risk of extinction, I decided that it would be interesting to try radiotronic communication with natural psychotransforming waves in search of capturing Les Vudu messages.

Inspired by Bertiaux's own accounts and slightly encouraged by a not-total lack of aptitude for drawing, I had decided that trying to encapsulate magical experiences through painting might be a good avenue for exploration. I had begun to capture these waves spread by reality and to decode them through simple magical operations, which impelled me to produce a canvas.

That afternoon, lost among so many others, I planned to do the same, and I thought everything would go as before. I would be stimulated by the waves, and I would pick up the communications and suddenly start painting something without any prior planning. However, on that particular afternoon, that's not exactly what happened.

I had begun to feel the physiological transformations triggered by the psychotransforming waves, and the radiotronic centers began to emit subtle Voodoo vibrations that echoed through my braincase and reverberated through my chest, stimulating the chakras to polarize in unison. However, despite these changes and the effects of altering consciousness and opening up subtle extrasensory vision, it seemed that either I wasn't picking up anything or I was not able to decode the things I picked up.

In my consciousness, at the ordinary level, operating in suppression by the weight of the upper layers, I was already beginning to believe that despite all the magical machinery being aligned, the operation would not succeed in producing a painting or even converting any comprehensible data.

After a while of keeping esoteric engineering operating, I decided it was time to take a little break. Still altered but out of any active receptive state, I headed to a specific room in the apartment looking for something. Upon entering the room, I came across a small spider clinging to the wall, those we commonly call flycatchers. It was facing me, at the level of my eyes, and staring at me. I was mesmerized and froze where I stood, dedicated to remaining in the exchange of glances. My two carnal eyes and my infinite astral eyes focused on the multiple visions the little arachnid had of me.

What could have sparked its interest in me? Was it my size? My humanoid form that seemed absurd to it? None of that! That spider was no ordinary arthropod. I didn't know it yet, but the psychotransforming waves had reached a certain level and the chakras were polarized in such a way that I had caught the attention of one of Les Vudu, who decided to pay me a visit. At my sign of reciprocity, the spider decided to teach me a secret. Spiders don't speak, at least not as we humans do, but they have many other features that can be readily read by those who know their language. At that moment I knew the arachnid language perfectly, a gift from Les Vudu. The spider began to make a series of movements with its legs, raising and lowering them in a certain rhythm and sequence. And I was standing there, gaping, watching her.

The spider's secret dance was another gift from Les Vudu and I understood immediately that the dance was a rite, a calling, a way to summon someone—Baron Zariguin!

The name exploded in my mind at the same time as a figure with an anthropomorphized arachnid face and top hat appeared. Its rather grayish keratin skin was a cross between a human and a spider's skull. His chelicerae or spider fangs jumped out from the corners of his open withered mouth, revealing yellowed teeth that seemed to compose an inhuman smile. What could the lwa of magic poisons, death, and time want with me? What did that spinner want to tell me anyway?

The spider had already delivered its message. In its dance it had given me a mission and a key. And here I had thought on that afternoon of oppression to the spirits, nothing would happen. . . .

Little did I know that I would be cast into an ancient mausoleum, taken over by webs and tiny crawling beings. For the mausoleum is the home of Baron Zariguin, the arachnid Ghuedhe, the one with eight legs. The one whose eyes glow in the darkness beyond time, like a constellation of troubled stars. The sinister weaver, whose silk will be our real shroud.

I ran to the canvas that was still waiting for my clumsy strokes from the paint-soaked brush and from it pulled out a portrait of the baron. Then I ended up (I'm not sure how) lying on the bed. Lying there, I began to chant a rudimentary mantra that echoed through the universes, telegraphing my desire for communication with the baron. How long I lay there, saying that impromptu prayer, I cannot say. Maybe it was a few minutes, but the notion of time no longer made sense. I was starting to penetrate timeless realities.

What can eternally lie is not dead, and in strange universes even time can die.*

Lines and geometric shapes invaded my astral vision—as if a weaver were pulling threads from there to here, in that phase of the creative process in which the work is still a blur. More squiggles and strange shapes were emerging and aggregating, like a great colony of small creatures they were coming together, bunching, turning, dancing, and vibrating until they found the right shape.

As clearly as you can see anything, I saw the *vèvè*—a Euclidean spider with its paws spread across the planes. It was then that I heard a voice that carried an unnerving radioactive force. I can't say where it came from or who it was or even what it was like. The voice came out as just a whisper, but soon the words bounced through the vibrations and found shelter in my consciousness.

Bawon Zariguin is he who spins the web of time and space. He enlarges and shortens it at his will. He can cut and even make a strand anew.

There is a secret dance to invoke the Bawon taught to me by a spider on the wall. It invites him to your head in order for him to show you it all.

The Bawon is the very dead and empty spaces and moments. Only through his legs one can voyage through them.

The Bawon wants me to tell you all that there is no such thing as a mere spider on the wall. Memento mori—but enjoy while you can! Because the Bawon will spin his web again!

---

*Inspired by H. P. Lovecraft.

His web is his very sister and consort so the Bawon is never alone.

You have to spin your own web. If you do so the Sorcery of Zaringuin will be straight ahead.

"You can call me to voyage or to sting. As a scorpion I'm a most poisonous thing. Try me if you dare. I believe you couldn't even stare. The Scorpion is a symbol of peril and pain. And this is what awaits those who would call me in vain."

I was at the center of the web of worlds, trapped in its most sinister side, the side commanded by Baron Zariguin. On the other side, in the face of life, his brother Anamse weaves threads of a different quality. It is the perpetual dance of these two that, like the beating of the universal heart, dictates the rhythm of people's days and nights and of everything else that exists.

There I was, being enveloped in their silk, not yet knowing that

Image 13.1. Bawon Zariguin. Photo by Eduardo Regis. For this image in color, see plate 9.

Anamse is always coordinated with his brother. While I was covered by threads and more threads and everything in me was transformed, Baron Zariguin injected Voodoo poisons, which made my eyes multiply like those of the arachnospirit itself. When I was completely and finally covered and was short of breath, I could see with my new eyes things that I could neither identify nor understand. Baron Zariguin's chelicerae were digging fiercely into my pineal, and all I could feel was the sting of metamorphosis, of Voodoo spider shape-shifting. The Atlantean secrets that traveled through my eyes and the incantations that were pronounced in my ears were all lost by the heat of the poisons and the transformation.

And when it was all over, I could hear the little legs walking through my mind. Tic, tic, tic, tic. The little legs going up and down, sewing short and long, straight and curvy strands.

Image 13.2. Baron Zariguin. Notebook sketch by Eduardo Regis.

14

The Work of Ordo Templi Orientis Antiqua and La Couleuvre Noire

Readers are certainly familiar with the concept of magical-esoteric orders. For this reason, it may seem futile to talk a little more about OTOA-LCN from an operative point of view. Let's start this discussion by making it extremely clear that the OTOA-LCN orders are not typical esoteric societies.

The Masonic structure, which by the manifestation of the Hermetic Order of the Golden Dawn ended up becoming the standard form in the organization of magical orders, does not apply in the present case. The idea of secret meetings, elaborate and quasi-theatrical temples, passwords, lengthy group rituals, and standardized instructions also does not define the OTOA-LCN orders. This is not to say that those elements cannot exist in the orders; of course they can. But that's just not how the orders are structured.

The first question we need to clarify is what exactly the two orders are and what the differences between them are. To discuss the OTOA we need to talk about the Monastery of the Seven Rays (M7R). The M7R is a school of occult teachings, a collective of portals, and a collective of magical consciousness. Although the M7R has a physical manifestation, obviously the real monastery cannot be reduced to that. We are not literally talking about an old building lost in a mountain range in some remote place. The monastery crosses universes but also connects them.

The best-known physical manifestation of the monastery is the teachings contained in the so-called four years of study in its curriculum. For many years these teachings were exclusive to OTOA members only. Recently, however, Bertiaux authorized the publication of part of this body of lessons for the general public in *Monastery of the Seven Rays: First Year Course* (2019) and some subsequent years. Therefore, interested readers may purchase a copy of part of these teachings. Studying these lessons should be more than enough to give you a good idea of what to expect from the order's magical work.

The OTOA is the collective of mages who connect through the many portals that exist in the infinite rooms of the monastery. It is the gathering of knowledge, experiments, experiences, and consciousnesses of these magicians and all the masters that form the M7R. This is the essence of OTOA.

The OTOA divides its members into sixteen degrees, and these are related to the Tree of Life, front and back. This innovation that communicates that the OTOA's exploratory universe is wider than that of most known magical orders is striking. In fact, *exploration*, as Frater Selwanga has already taught, is the word that best defines the operative work of the order.[1]

The monastery is, in fact, a great school or a great laboratory. In it, mages can dedicate themselves to Vudotronic engineering, Zothyrian physics, and any other area that interests them. There are no taboos and no limits to the areas that can be worked on. Each member of the OTOA is a universe of his own, full of possibilities and very particular configurations. The monastery will present itself in a unique way to each of its members.

It is evident that the lessons contained in the monastery as well as the practices must be studied and considered by every member of the

OTOA. Without that, without this fundamental introduction to the system, the member will be left without a solid foundation to jump into her own future explorations. In this sense, the lessons of the M7R must be seen for what they are: invaluable instructions aimed at preparing the mage for his own particular journey.

The teachings of the Monastery of the Seven Rays fall within what we might call the Voudon Gnostic current, but if an explorer wishes to venture deeper into this system, he may find what he is looking for at La Couleuvre Noire. LCN is a sister order of the OTOA, whose interest is in unraveling and working out certain mysteries of the Voudon Gnostic current. In fact, OTOA and LCN would be better described as Siamese twins. Both orders are born from the same cauldron of influences and from the same person's hands, and they mix strongly, although they have distinct flavors of their own.

Generally speaking, an OTOA member will also be a member of LCN. This is the best way to communicate how the work of the two orders is intertwined. In other words, the explorer will be immersed in the same current, the current of the Voudon Gnostic system, when working in one or the other, and therefore, this "mixing" of the two ends up taking place. However, LCN has its own structure and a separate grade system, divided into four grades. That is, it has particular mysteries that require autonomy. This stems from the fact that LCN has closer links with Haitian Vodou secret societies, while the OTOA is more on the side of European initiatory orders. Therefore, even though Lucien François Jean-Maine built the two orders from the same matrix of influences in their genesis, they ended up being built with slightly different personalities. The OTOA takes more from the OTO source of Reuss, P. B. Randolph, and other currents of the Western esoteric tradition, while LCN structures itself from a secret society of Haitian Vodou.

These secret societies are initiatory groups with marked structures, often based on military organization. Generally, they deal with Vodou spirits that are considered aggressive and dangerous, and they enjoy enormous respect in Haiti because of the magical powers attributed to their members. An example of these societies is the Bizango, very famous for being a warlike society and for using human skulls to make figures of magical warriors. LCN derives from a not-so-well-known secret society, which would be responsible for the defense of Haiti and whose members would be recognized by the barely perceptible tattoos of black snakes on their heads.

One of the most interesting things about these societies is that they develop a very particular form of Haitian Vodou, focused on certain spirits that are their patrons, according to their nature and interest. Thus, the ceremonies and the very understanding of the Vodou cosmovision can be quite diverse within these societies. With this in mind, we can begin to understand exactly where the Haitian roots of the Voudon Gnostic current run.

This explains why we constantly refer to orders as a single organism (OTOA-LCN). In fact, they are very close, both at the base and in the spirit of exploration and freedom.

I hope that readers have understood more clearly the nature, purpose, and work of these orders. The emphasis on the exploratory character is certainly the great differential of the OTOA-LCN operative vein. However, this demands a serious and committed work from the magician because only then will it be possible to masterfully navigate the paths of our universes.

15

Working with Les Vudu

The Voudon Gnostic Workbook is essentially a practice book. It is full of lessons with suggestions for operations, reflections, studies, and so on. There is no better source than Bertiaux himself to delve deeply into the world of Voudon Gnosticism. But I can suggest one or another practice that will give you an idea of what it is like to navigate the waters of this system.

What follows are some simple practices that will help you get in touch with the spirits of Hoo and Doo and with other Les Vudu. Almost all of the practices described here involve the construction of simple magical machines. Feel free to adapt the materials to your situation and the materials you have at hand. Remember that one of the great advantages of the Voudon Gnostic system is its versatility.

✧ Practice 1: Voudonist Guia

The *guia* is a necklace made by the Voudon Gnostic with the aim of capturing and concentrating the Voudonist radiations emitted by the spirits. There are many uses for these necklaces, but the main one, of course, is to assist in rituals and operations, acting as a magnet for unseen spiritual powers.

Making a guia is very easy. You can dedicate it to any spirit or group of spirits. In this initial phase, we will make a guia dedicated to the spirits of

Hoo and Doo. You will need, at a minimum, the following materials:

- Nylon or cotton thread
- Assorted beads in a variety of colors
- Pendants depicting marine elements, such as aquatic animals and shells, and death elements, such as coffins, skulls, and so on
- Black candle
- Chalk or pen and paper

In your imagination, visualize your guia. How will it be arranged? Will the beads be distributed into groups of marine and death elements or randomly? Will you use green or blue beads to represent water or both? What about death? Perhaps black and violet beads? Meditate for as long as necessary until the guia appears in your inner vision. While meditating, chant the following mantra: *May the spirits of Hoo and Doo help me.*

To assemble the guia, first get a general idea of how long you would like it to be. It is important that the necklace, when hung around the neck, does not limit movements, and also that it is not uncomfortable. Calculate the approximate amount of string and beads and pendants you should use and make sure you have enough material. I recommend that you first unspool the thread and string the beads and pendants before cutting the thread, so that you can make adjustments.

Arrange the beads and pendants according to your vision. Check if the size of the guia is adequate. If everything is right, cut the thread and make a knot: your guia is ready.

Put it around your neck and with the chalk trace a cross on the floor. Alternatively, make a cross on paper. Place the black candle in the center of the cross. Light the candle and repeat:

Lucky Hoodoo Spirits, I have made the guia as you instructed me, and now I ask you to magnetize it with your spiritual powers. May this guia serve as a link between us.

Remove the guia from your neck and place it at the foot of the candle. Let the candle burn down completely. You will then be in possession of a powerful esoteric machine. See color plate 10 and plate 11.

✧ Practice 2: The Hoodoo Altar

Now let's set up a small Hoodoo altar, in which you will perform esoteric prayers and other rituals. (See color plate 12.)

The minimum materials needed are:

- Wooden board measuring approximately thirty centimeters by thirty centimeters (about twelve inches square)
- Pen
- Paints of various colors and brushes
- Five candles: black, red, blue, green, and yellow
- Guia

Put on your Voudonist guia and declare the following to the universe:

May the spirits of Hoodoo hear my call and lend me their vision for a new altar to be erected.

Take a deep breath, sit down with all the materials around you, and close your eyes. Again, first build the altar in your imagination. The spirits will communicate to you the signs, words, and images that you need to paint on your personal altar.

First, draw the signs and images in ink and paint in the colors as you saw in your vision. It doesn't matter if you are particularly talented or not for painting and drawing. Do the best you can and as you feel you must. If you are inspired to add other decorations, like stones, beads, and pictures, feel free. If the instruction to do so comes, and you do not have the necessary materials at hand, store the altar in a safe place and return to work on it at another time, after obtaining what you need.

Once the altar is finished, allow the paint to dry for a day. The following night, put on your guia and arrange the candles on the altar in the following order: black candle in the middle, blue candle in the west, yellow in the north, red in the east, and green in the south. Light the yellow candle first and then the others in an anticlockwise direction until you reach the east. Finally, light the black candle and close your eyes and say:

Spirits of Hoo and Doo come bless the new altar erected.

Feel the arrival of the spirits of Hoo and Doo. Notice the different sensations that each group brings. When you are sure the spirits have arrived, say:

I offer this altar to you so that our relationship may be harmonious and fruitful. The powers of light drive the darkness away and I know you are my friends.

Stay in a meditative state for a few minutes. Maybe they want to send a message or make themselves present in some way. Notice the whole environment and be aware of the signs. When you feel you have received their communications, extinguish the candles in the reverse order in which they were lit and say:

I bid farewell to the spirits of Hoodoo and thank them for being here today.

✧ Practice 3: The Atua

The *atua*, often a magical box, is a more stable and lasting repository or seat for spirits. (See color plate 13.) You should only build it if you are willing to maintain a deeper and more constant relationship with the invisible. Having one at home will attract many blessings from the spirits, but it is also a responsibility as it is a declaration of commitment. If you don't feel ready to make this decision, skip ahead to the next practice.

The most traditional way to create an atua is to use a wooden box. To set up an atua for the spirits of Hoo and Doo, you will need:

- Wooden box of good quality big enough to accommodate two images or figures; avoid cheap wood, such as plywood
- Paint, brushes, and other craft materials
- Black candle
- Image or figure of an aquatic animal, preferably fish, turtle, snake, or frog
- Image or figure of something related to death and the cemetery, such as skull, coffin, skeleton, and so on
- Guia
- Altar, with its five candles

Wear your guia, prepare your altar, light the candles, and declare:

Spirits of Hoodoo, I will build an atua for you to bless my home, my temple and to strengthen our relationship. Please teach me how.

Again, get into a meditative state and build the atua in your imagination. Notice the drawings, signs, and symbols that must be drawn or painted on the box. After this step, paint the box and decorate it and then say:

The box is almost ready; I ask that the spirits now do their part.

Extinguish the candles on the altar, as instructed in the previous practice, collect them, and put them away. Place the box next to the altar and let it dry completely for a day. In the meantime, the spirits will make astral preparations for the atua.

The following night, after the paint has completely dried, put on your guia and light the five candles on your altar again. Inside the atua, place the two images or figures with the black candle in the middle. Light the candle saying:

Spirits of Hoodoo, may you feel that this atua is a suitable and pleasant home. Come and live here, this is my request.

Leave the temple but be sure that the candles and box are safely away from flammable materials, and go check on them intermittently. Let the candles burn down completely. The next morning, the atua will be loaded and ready. You can use it to bring luck and favors from the spirits to your home or use it as a magical magnetizing machine. For example, put requests written on paper inside the atua so that the spirits can answer them, or place objects in the box to charge them with the energies of Hoodoo. See color plate 14.

✧ Practice 4: Receiving Voudonist Messages

This practice is very important to open up your experimental field. If you are not comfortable building an atua, this fourth practice will help you communicate with the spirits and build a relationship with them. In any case, any Voudon Gnostic will benefit from this practice, and I recommend that everyone do it from time to time.

Necessary materials:

- Small notebook
- Paper and pen, colored pencils, colored pens

Wear your guia and light your altar. Sit in front of the altar and begin an esoteric prayer process: in other words, start talking to the spirits. If you are unable to connect in this way, use the names of the spirits as a mantra. For example, in the case of Hoodoo spirits, the mantra would be *Hoodoo*. Repeat the word until exhaustion. This should be enough for a slight change in consciousness, which will transform your mind into a Voodoo antenna capable of capturing the vibrations that were hidden until then.

Then, yield to Les Vudu urges emitted by the altar and from the guia. Let yourself be carried away in astral and imaginative visions. Hear voices, see pictures, have ideas. Nothing is impossible in that state. Draw, annotate, and write down all the messages you receive. Worry about deciphering their meanings later.

✧ Practice 5: Sexual Voodoo Energy Use Training

This is an entry-level practice based on Luc Guzotte's practices, which are described in the VGW. To perform this work, I advise the use of either a yoga mat or a meditation chair.

Sit in the lotus position or lie on the yoga mat. Get comfortable and close your eyes. Take three deep breaths and then breathe in your natural rhythm until you feel very relaxed. Think of a goal or object that is particularly interesting to you. It could be anything: improving in studies, learning a new skill, solving a problem. It does not matter. Leave that goal or object imprinted in consciousness, but place it on a layer below by bringing something else to your attention, in this case by imagining one or more sexual objects that interest you. Start visualizing the most diverse erotic situations. Allow the erotic energies to palpably grow and expand. Take your time. Don't be in a hurry.

When you feel that enough erotic energy has been circulated, bring back to mind the object or goal you desire and visualize yourself sending all that erotic energy to it. You may, for example, visualize sexual rays going from your body to the object. Do this until you feel empty of erotic energy. Repeat this training as many times as necessary.

Remember that when we desire something, we can polarize ourselves in a way that attracts our desires through the circulation and emission of sexual energy. This is precisely what this practice is intended to train.

Acknowledgments

I would like to thank my wife, Andrea, for all her support in all my matters spiritual and magical. I am most grateful, too, to my sisters and brothers in the OTOA-LCN family, especially Katy, Alu, and Sean Woodward and, of course, Frater Selwanga. I extend my acknowledgment to Nicholaj de Mattos Frisvold for his amazing and very informative foreword and also for Sébastien de la Croix for his incredible contribution. Also, I must thank Diego de Oxóssi from Arolê Cultural, and Chris Cappelluti, Kate Mueller, and all the people at Inner Traditions for their awesome work on the book. Finally, I thank Diógenes Costa for making the picture of Bertiaux and Jean-Maine for this book.

The Universe of a Wandering Gnostic Monastery in the Voudon Gnostic Multiverse: A Brief Review of Tau Palamas's Work

Sébastien de la Croix

Those who make contact with the Voudon Gnostic current for the first time often find the system impenetrable and difficult to follow, mainly because it does not readily reveal itself: the theoretical and practical materials of the Monastery of the Seven Rays, of the OTOA, of LCN, and, in particular, from *The Voudon Gnostic Workbook* are usually understood as a closed system, albeit vast, deep, and complex. It takes some time for the student to understand that, far from being cookbooks, these guides are just the starting point for the elaboration of an intimate, very personal Gnostic magical system, endowed with the unique signature of the practitioner.

Perhaps the best picture to express the nature of this multifaceted universe of Voudon Gnosticism is the kaleidoscope, that toy, now somewhat outdated, that, by means of mirrors and bits of colored glass, allows the creation of virtually infinite multicolored geometric patterns. Just as the mirrors inside the kaleidoscope are fixed, so too are the structural pillars of the system, all of which are based on the sixteen *méjì odù* of Ifá; just as the tiny pieces of multicolored glass are mobile, so are their constitutive elements, although always integrated into a perfect, mathematically identifiable pattern. These sixteen pairs of *odù*, which are the portals of creation through which everything comes into being, have a parallel in the Gnostic syzygies, the pairs of aeons which, in turn, will compose and sustain the *Ecclesia Gnostica Spiritualis*.

Michael Bertiaux, in his writings, never stopped emphasizing that the current of Voudon Gnosticism is the science of elaboration and construction of the temple of consciousness, created by the mind fed by will and imagination. To this end, the guidelines of the Voudon Gnostic system will serve to guide the student and magician in organizing his inner experience of a Gnostic and magical nature, through the symbols that are most appropriate and familiar to him, as it will be precisely these symbols that will have the greatest power for the operator, becoming veritable machines that generate magical power. In other words, the system's internal contacts or lwas will manifest through these symbols, no matter what they are.[1]

In *The Voudon Gnostic Workbook*, when addressing the Monastery of the Seven Rays as "the Catholic and magickal department of modern gnostic consciousness," Bertiaux emphasizes that any structured series of magical operations can be created by the practitioner in any situation, giving as possible examples of this superlatively flexible experimentation a Voodoo Gnosticism, and a Jungian Gnosticism, along with Thelemic, Catholic, Zothyrian, and Enochian influences, among other endless possibilities. To this end, "an infinite number of magickal entities can be contacted," using the scale of sixteen double patterns already mentioned, as it will ensure harmony among elements that are apparently disparate and strange to each other.[2]

As Frater Vameri observes in this work, which the reader has in his hands, "there are no taboos and no limits to the areas that can be worked on," since "each member of the OTOA is a universe of his own, full of possibilities and very particular configurations," so that "the monastery will present itself in a unique way to each of its members." However, although this teaching constitutes a precious *key* that is not usually given to the student in this clear and objective way, the doubt may remain about how to undertake this unique, particular work, in this multiverse of infinite possibilities.

It is precisely about an exquisite example of construction of a personal magical system based on the current of Vodoun Gnosticism that I intend to discuss in this appendix: the work of Tau Palamas, *Syzygy: Reflections on the Monastery of the Seven Rays*, in which the entire theoretical and practical structure of a monastery of Gnostic *gyrovagues*, that is, of wandering monks, not physically fixed in a certain place nor belonging to a certain Catholic religious order, is exposed. The proposal, as can be seen at first, is doubly heretical: on the one hand, it is ostensibly Gnostic though not dualistic, a "heresy" that has always been fought by the Roman Catholic Church, and on the other hand, it is structured in the spirit of the gyrovagues, who were harshly criticized by Saint Benedict himself and were prohibited by the Councils of Chalcedon (fifth century) and the Second Council of Nicaea (eighth century).

Tau Palamas, echoing Bertiaux's lessons, starts from the premise that there is an incalculable multiplicity of plans in the Monastery of the Seven Rays, allowing each of its members to have a unique experience. In his own words:

[T]he Monastery of the Seven Rays is a holistic empire, divinizing all aspects of our existence and sending us outward into the multiverses and secret spaces laid out for us on our unique travels upon the Gran Chemin (the Great Way). The Monastery is no stale Order of mimicry, demanding its postulants live a life of following others' words, praying before others' Icons and worshipping others' ideas of Deity. Our Monastery demands participation, work and a mind that is free and thinks for itself. Each of our individual ontic spheres acts as a morphic field which, when in resonation with another's field (spiritually or physically), causes *genesis* and *genius* to be born and creates a powerful upsurge of creative force and energy.[3]

Each individual journey through the Gran Chemin leads to an individual Gnostic space, and it is his particular Gnostic locus that Tau Palamas presents in the work being discussed here, a locus inhabited by itinerant Gnostic (nondual) Christian monks. Tau Palamas defines himself as a Christian bishop at the service of a Christian community, stressing that, initially, he approached the Catholic saints, especially Saint Gregory Palamas, from whom the strength of the lwas was expressed. This fact is not surprising, since in Haitian Vodou, as well as in the oldest Umbanda in Brazil, there is not exactly a syncretism between saints and lwas, as understood by the concealment of the non-Christian divinity under the mask of the Catholic saint, but rather a symbiosis, amalgamation, or even transfiguration between the saint and the lwa. As Tau Palamas emphasizes, the spiritual realm does not translate into a closed system, and "the energies will take on whatever form we are working with, this is why practitioners may even make use of Lovecraftian magick in our system."[4]

The work is divided into two parts, one theoretical, *ora*, and the other practical, *labora*—composing the traditional Benedictine, alchemical, and Rosicrucian motto: *ora et labora*. In the rich theoretical section of the book, the author begins by explaining the need to cultivate mental tranquility as a prerequisite for healing and adjusting body and soul—*aeques animus*. For this purpose, the use of the psalms constitutes a very important working tool—*opus dei*—either because of its profoundly theurgic character or because of its oracular aspect as a book of bibliomancy par excellence. Moreover, found in all known mystical traditions (*mantra*, *anussati*, *zikr*), the remembrance of the divine names present in the psalms leads the practitioner to the silence that precedes the mystical communion, in which the lover and the beloved merge in pure love.

Then follows the *Lectio Divina*, the meditating and meditative reading of the scriptures (in which the lessons of the Monastery of the Seven Rays are inserted), which is not dissociated from the daily encounter with the spirits, whose whispering voices are heard while savoring the gnosis extracted from the text. Therefore, with regard to the lessons of the Monastery of the Seven Rays, it is necessary to allow the essence of the text to penetrate one's own soul, ruminating the text tirelessly, so that it becomes a bridge through which the spirits can pass.

All these steps of this very particular monastic path lead to the superior triangle formed by prayer (*oratio*), contemplation (*contemplati*), and enlightenment (*illuminatio*), not necessarily in that order, leading to silent union with the spirits and the awakening of psychic abilities such as clairvoyance and clairaudience. A synthesis of this mystical work, which is nothing more than the Communion of Saints mentioned in the Apostles' Creed of the Roman Catholic Church, can be found in the technique of esoteric prayer taught in *The Voudon Gnostic Workbook*.

The most important obstacle to overcome to achieve this communion is to get rid of the belief that spirits are very far from us, in unreachable places on some sublime plane. On the contrary, it is enough for us to silence our mind, to enter our particular Gnostic space, to find them always waiting for us. As Tau Palamas explains:

> Spirits and Masters await our approach, the Great Communion of Saints are constantly at the ready, the Lwa and primordial currents take shape and form during esoteric prayer and souldreams, and the true Elders of our Monastery become living vehicles into Otherwhere. Those same Teachers, when we place ourselves under their tutelage, can offer precise initiations that coincide with our

particular needs and developments. Holy Listening is essential to discern such subtle vibrations.[5]

Michael Bertiaux presents the same idea in the preface to *The Voudon Gnostic Workbook*, stating that "when using esoteric prayer, what you do is talk to the spirits as if they were sitting next to you. . . . They are always ready to listen to us."[6] However, this listening to the spirits does not always happen by clairaudience, but many times it is processed as impressions analogous to the passes* experienced in the operations of the Élus-Cöens by Martinez de Pasqually or even as dreams, in which the highest initiations into the Gnostic realms take place.

Tau Palamas, still regarding esoteric prayer as a tool to propitiate the communion of saints, warns that "it is not enough to simply present tobacco and rum, the correctly drawn veves and such to the Lwa—it is not enough to say a few prayers to the Saints and light the appropriate colored candle—we must to talk to the Spirits."[7] The real power, as it turns out, is in simplicity, and this is a huge challenge for the practitioner, especially due to the contemporary Western mentality that advocates that only what is achieved through a lot of effort or through complex technologies is worth it.

The practical lesson that can be extracted from just these brief excerpts collected from the writings of Palamas and Bertiaux is quite relevant and deserves to be emphasized: in the domains of Western magic or Afro-diasporic faiths, whatever they may be, contact with spirits or invisible beings is essentially done mechanically, bureaucratically, or in a petitionary way, reproducing the Christian pattern of petitioning God, Christ, and the saints. Although this approach is the simplest, very few dedicate themselves to talking to the spirits and even fewer to listening to them. People are taught to communicate with the invisible

---

*"Passes" are strange, otherwise-unaccounted-for phenomena like detectable perfumes or other scents, blinking lights, or even the sigils of certain spirits appearing in thin air.

in these mechanical, excessively ceremonial ways, but they are no longer taught how to cultivate the inner silence that would encourage them to *listen* to subtle feelings and messages.

But this work by Tau Palamas is not limited to the highest and most subtle ontic spheres in the context of Gnostic Christian Voudon, but also to the domain of the palpable, of the corporeal, where there will be practices involving points-chauds and ojas, because the physical body is where all the mysteries are found. The practice is both transcendent and immanent, and in the latter aspect, it turns to the recognition of the divine presence in the multiplicity of forms. For nondualist Gnosticism, the body is sacred, and sexual magic itself has a dimension that goes far beyond the merely physical plane. It is only through the use of the physical body and with the help of the physical body that the deification (*deificatio*) described by Saint Athanasius, the sole goal of all humanity, can be achieved.

In this context of integration of the physical body in the process of deification, the Ghuedhe spirits cannot be left out, as those who have gone before not only support and guide us, but also express the fear of oblivion and the extinction of ourselves, inherent in human nature. And that fear needs to be faced bravely. It is precisely for this reason that the dead must be remembered and worshipped (*memento mori*), and this is where some macabre and horrifying aspects of the lessons of *The Voudon Gnostic Workbook* fit in and justify themselves. The adept needs to work so hard on this dark side that there is no authentic spiritual tradition that does not have this tool, be it composed of the angry deities and protectors of the dharma of Buddhism, the tantric rites in crematoria with libations on human skulls, or the chapels and Christian churches covered by hundreds of human skeletons. Examples of this are the Trappists, who greet each other by saying *memento mori* and have a human skull among their meager possessions, or the crypt of the Capuchin friars in Rome, decorated with more than four thousand human bones.

The second part of the work is, at the same time, a Christian breviary and a magical grimoire. It comprises guidelines for structuring an oratory, with a specific exorcism for the objects displayed therein, and a Christian oblation ritual adapted from the ritualistic technology of OTOA and LCN, in which the practitioner dedicates himself to the Monastery of the Seven Rays and the spirits that integrate it. This is followed by a breviary with prayers for the different parts of the day, in a Liturgy of the Hours adapted to this particular modality of work.

Crowning the practical part of the wandering monastery of Tau Palamas is a method of contacting the personal patron saint from a set of sixteen saints correlated with the Vodou lwas and their characteristic colors, as well as precise instructions for invoking them. Finally, closing his Christian Gnostic grimoire with a golden key, Tau Palamas suggests the theurgic work with sixteen psalms, in a construct derived from the traditional use of psalms in Hoodoo that resumes a very powerful magical tradition, but somewhat forgotten nowadays in favor of "novelties" of rather questionable effectiveness. Thus, it is evident that Tau Palamas fashioned a profoundly unique and enigmatic magical and mystical realm in contrast to the more widely recognized universe depicted by Michael Bertiaux in *The Voudon Gnostic Workbook*. This serves to substantiate Bertiaux's proposition that Voudon Gnosticism entails the intricate creation of one's own realm of consciousness by harnessing the powers of will and imagination—a concept originally posited by Éliphas Lévi during the latter part of the nineteenth century. And all of this, laced with a touch of irony: Palamas brought forth a Christian magical universe that undoubtedly intrigued those who assume that Vodou, and especially Voudon Gnosticism, must inherently be dark, obscure, and sinister.

Sébastien de la Croix is the coauthor with Diamantino Fernandes Trindade of *Vodou, Voodoo, and Hoodoo: Explore the Evolution of Caribbean Magic*, to be published in 2024. He is a houngan of Haitian Vodou, a researcher, and practitioner of Afro-Brazilian religions. He is also a priest of Umbanda and Quimbanda and is the head of a *Quimbanda de raiz tradicional* (Root Traditional Quimbanda) in Minas Geraiz, Brazil.

Notes

FOREWORD.
GNOSTIC VÛDÛ: AN INTRODUCTION

1. Bertiaux, *Ontological Grafitti*, 126.
2. Bertiaux, *Voudon Gnostic Workbook*, 266.

CHAPTER 1.
THE FOUNDATION: HISTORY AND MYTH

1. Bertiaux, "Arts and the Occult: An Interview with Michael Bertiaux."

CHAPTER 7.
ZOTHYRIA BEYOND THE STARS:
INSIDE YOUR MIND

1. Bertiaux, *Voudon Gnostic Workbook*, 270.
2. Bailey, *The Labours of Hercules: An Astrological Interpretation*, 47–48.

CHAPTER 8.
THE SERPENT AND THE EGG: COSMIC SEXUAL MAGIC

1. Couliano, *Eros and Magic in the Renaissance*, 5, 76.
2. Couliano, 88.
3. Randolph and Naglowska, *Magia Sexualis*, 34.

CHAPTER 10.
THE MAGICAL-SPIRITUAL SESSIONS OF HYDE PARK LODGE

1. Morton, *Calling the Spirits*, 12.
2. Morton, 118, 120.
3. Morton, 121.
4. Morton, 125.
5. Morton, 128.
6. Morton, 130.
7. Morton, 138.
8. Morton, 196.
9. Bertiaux, *Ontological Graffiti*, 19.
10. Bertiaux, 25.
11. Bertiaux, 89.

CHAPTER 14.
THE WORK OF ORDO TEMPLI ORIENTIS ANTIQUA
AND LA COULEUVRE NOIRE

1. "OTOA e Thelema," OTOA-LCN Brazil website.

APPENDIX.
THE UNIVERSE OF A WANDERING GNOSTIC MONASTERY
IN THE VOUDON GNOSTIC MULTIVERSE:
A BRIEF REVIEW OF TAU PALAMAS'S WORK

1. Bertiaux, "Course in Esoteric Voudoo," Scribd.
2. Bertiaux, *Voudon Gnostic Workbook*, 75.
3. Palamas, *Syzygy*, 23, 36.
4. Palamas, 83.
5. Palamas, 66.
6. Palamas, iii.
7. Palamas, 83.

Bibliography

Ackermann, Hans W., Maryse Gautier, and Michel-Ange Momplaisir. *Les Esprits du Vodou Haitien*. Pompano Beach, FL.: Educa Vision, 2010.

Bailey, Alice A. *The Labours of Hercules: An Astrological Interpretation*. New York: Lucis, 2011.

Bascom, William. *Ifa Divintaion: Communication between Gods and Men in West Africa*. Bloomington: Indiana University Press, 1991.

Beabrun, Mimerose. *Nan Domi: An Initiate's Journey into Haitian Vodou*. Translated by D. J. Walker. San Francisco: City Lights Books, 2013.

Bertiaux, Michael. "Arts and the Occult: An Interview with Michael Bertiaux," interview by B. S. Pedersen. Academia, 2003.

———. *Cagliostro: The Secret Lives*. 3 vols. Milan, Italy: Media Print Editore, 2021–2022.

———. "Course in Esoteric Voodoo," 1977.

———. "Meeting Le Maitr," interview by A. Van de Voorde. Fulgur, n.d.

———. *Monastery of the Seven Rays: First Year Course*. Milan, Italy: Media Print Editore, 2019.

———. *Ontological Graffiti*. Somerset, UK: Fulgur, 2016.

———. *The Voudon Gnostic Workbook*. Expanded ed. San Francisco: Weiser Books, 2007. First published 1988.

———. *Vûdû Cartography*. Somerset, UK: Fulgur, 2010.

Blavatsky, Helena Petrovna. *The Secret Doctrine*. 2 vols. Pasedena, CA: Theosophical University Press, 2014. First published 1893.

Carr, David. "Kant, Husserl, and the Nonempirical Ego." *Journal of Philosophy* 74, no. 11 (1970): 682–90.

Côrrea, Ivan. *Teodicéia Psíquica*. São Paulo, Brazil: Daemon Editora, 2021.

Costa, Marcos R. N. *Maniqueísmo. História, Filosofia e Religião*. Rio de Janeiro, Brazil: Editora Vozes, 2000.

Couliano, Ioan P. *Eros and Magic in the Renaissance*. Chicago: University of Chicago Press, 1987.

Croix, Sébastien de la, and Trindade, D. F. *Vodou, Voodoo, and Hoodoo: Explore the Evolution of Caribbean Magic*. Woodbury, MN: Llewellyn, 2024.

Crowley, Aleister. *Magick: Liber ABA, Book 4*. San Francisco: Weiser Books, 1998.

Deren, Maya. *Divine Horsemen: The Living Gods of Haiti*. Kingston, NY: McPherson, 1985.

Drury, Nevill. *Stealing Fire from Heaven: The Rise of Modern Western Magic*. New York: Oxford University Press, 2011.

Duquette, Lon M. *The Chicken Qabalah of Rabbi Lamed Ben Clifford: Dilettante's Guide to What You Do and Do Not Need to Know to Become a Qabalist*. San Francisco: Weiser Books, 2001.

Eliade, Mircea. *Tratado de História das Religiões*. São Paulo, Brazil: WMF Martins Fontes, 2016.

Fite, Kyle. *Hoodoo Pilot*. Cali, Colombia: Sirius Limited Esoterica, 2020.

Fortune, Dion. *The Mystical Qabalah*. San Francisco: Weiser Books, 2022. First published 1984 in Portuguese.

Frisvold, Nicholaj de M. *Exu and the Quimbanda of Night and Fire*. London: Scarlet Imprint, 2016.

———. *Invisible Fire: Inner Dimensions of Western Gnostic and Theurgic Tradition*. Somerset, UK: Capall Bann, 2010.

———. *Palo Mayombe: The Garden of Blood and Bones*. London: Scarlet Imprint, 2016.

———. *Pomba Gira and the Quimbanda of Mbumba Nzila*. London: Scarlet Imprint, 2011.

Grant, Kenneth. *Cults of the Shadow*. London: Starfire, 1975.

Guaita, Stanislas O. de. *Templo de Satã*. 2 vols. São Paulo, Brazil: Biblioteca Planeta, Editora Três, 1973.

Heidegger, Martin. *Ser e Tempo*. Rio de Janeiro, Brazil: Editora Vozes, 2015.

Hine, Phil. *Pseudonomicon*. Tempe, AZ: Original Falcon Press, 2009.

Hoeller, Stephan A. *Gnosticism: New Light on the Ancient Tradition of Inner Knowing*. Wheaton, IL: Quest Books, 2002.

Husserl, Edmund A. *Ideia da Femonologia: Cinco Lições*. Rio de Janeiro, Brazil: Editora Vozes, 2020.

LaMenfo, Mambo V. Z. K. *Serving the Spirits: The Religion of Haitian Vodou*. Independently published, 2011.

Lévi, Éliphas. *Dogma e Ritual da Alta Magia*. São Paulo, Brazil: Editora Pensamento, 2017.

Marcondes, Danilo. *Iniciação à História da Filosofia: Dos Pré-socráticos a Wittgenstein*. Rio de Janeiro, Brazil: Zahar, 1997.

Maupoil, Bernard A. *Advinhação na Antiga Costa dos Escravos*. São Paulo, Brazil: Edusp, 2017.

Morton, Lisa. *Calling the Spirits: A History of Seances*. London: Reaktion Books, 2020.

Otto, Rudolf. *O Sagrado*. São Leopoldo, Brazil: Sinodal, 2014.

Oxóssi, Diego de. *Desvendando Exu: O Guardião dos Caminhos*. São Paulo, Brazil: Arolê Cultural, 2018.

———. *Traditional Brazilian Black Magic: The Secrets of the Kimbanda Magicians*. Rochester, VT: Destiny Books, 2021.

Palamas, Tau. *Syzygy: Reflections on the Monastery of the Seven Rays*. West Yorkshire, UK: Hadean, 2013.

Papus (Gérard Encausse). *Tratado Elementar de Magia Prática*. São Paulo, Brazil: Editora Pensamento, 1978.

Parés, Luis N. *The Formation of Candomblé: Vodun History and Ritual in Brazil*. Translated by R. Vernon. Chapel Hill: University of North Carolina Press, 2013.

———. *O Rei, o Pai e a Morte*. São Paulo, Brazil: Companhia das Letras, 2016.

Pasqually, Martinès de. *Treatise on the Reintegration of Beings: In Their First Spiritual Divine Property, Virtue, and Power*. Translated by Felix M. Longji. Meadville, PA: Christian Faith, 2019. First published 1773.

Randolph, Paschal B., and Maria de Naglowska. *Magia Sexualis: Sexual Practices for Magical Power*. Rochester, VT: Inner Traditions, 2012.

Regardie, Israel. *The Golden Dawn: The Original Account of the Teachings, Rites and Ceremonies of the Hermetic Order*. Woodbury, MN: Llewellyn, 2016.

Regis, Eduardo. *Vodou Haitiano: Serviço aos Lwas*. São Paulo, Brazil: Daemon Editora, Selo Espelho de Circe, 2022.

Rigaud, Milo. *Secrets of Voodoo*. Translated by R. Cross. San Francisco: City Lights Books, 2016.

———. *Ve-ve: Diagrammes rituels du Voudou*. New York: French and European Publications, 1974.

Roggemans, Marcel. *History of Martinism and the F.U.D.O.S.I.* Translated by M. Bogaard. Lulu.com, 2009.

Römer, Thomas. *The Invention of God.* Cambridge, MA: Harvard University Press, 2015.

———. *A Origem de Javé: O Deus de Israel e seu Nome.* São Paulo, Brazil: Paulus Editora, 2016.

Smoley, Richard. *Forbidden Faith: The Gnostic Legacy from the Gospels to the Da Vinci Code.* New York: HarperOne, 2006.

———. *Gnosticismo: Esoterismo e Magia.* São Paulo, Brazil: Madras, 2019.

Tallant, Robert. *Voodoo in New Orleans.* New Orleans: Pelican, 1994.

Tann, Mambo C. *Haitian Vodou: An Introduction to Haiti's Indigenous Spiritual Tradition.* Woodbury, MN: Llewellyn, 2012.

Trindade, Diamantino F., Rolando A. Linares, and Wagner V. Costa. *Os Orixás na Umbanda e no Candomblé.* São Paulo, Brazil: Madras, 2014.

Trindade, Diamantino F., and Sebastien de la Croix. *Vodu, Voodoo e Hoodoo: A Magia do Caribe e o Império de Marie Laveau.* São Paulo, Brazil: Arolê Cultural, 2021.

Wang, Robert O. *The Qabalistic Tarot Book: A Textbook of Mystical Philosophy.* Stamford, CT: U.S. Games Systems, 2017. First published 1998 in Portuguese.

Woodward, Sean. *Keys to the Hoodoo Kingdom.* Independently published, 2017.

Zandee, J. "Gnostics Ideas on the Fall and Salvation." *Numen* 11, no. 1 (1964): 13–74.

Index